GEORGE V

The Guided Tour Series

Anne Bradstreet: A Guided Tour of the Life and Thought of a Puritan Poet, by Heidi L. Nichols

George Whitefield: A Guided Tour of His Life and Thought, by James L. Schwenk

J. Gresham Machen: A Guided Tour of His Life and Thought, by Stephen J. Nichols

Jonathan Edwards: A Guided Tour of His Life and Thought, by Stephen J. Nichols

Katherine Parr: A Guided Tour of the Life and Thought of a Reformation Queen, by Brandon G. Withrow

Martin Luther: A Guided Tour of His Life and Thought, by Stephen J. Nichols

Pages from Church History: A Guided Tour of Christian Classics, by Stephen J. Nichols

Thomas Manton: A Guided Tour of the Life and Thought of a Puritan Pastor, by Derek Cooper

Other Church History Books in the Guided Tour Series

Princeton Seminary (1812–1929): Its Leaders' Lives and Works, by Gary Steward

Stephen J. Nichols, series editor

GEORGE WHITEFIELD

A Guided Tour of His Life and Thought

JAMES L. SCHWENK

P&R PUBLISHING
P.O. BOX 817 • PHILLIPSBURG • NEW JERSEY 08865-0817

Scripture quotations in Whitefield's text are from the King James Version, sometimes rendered loosely from memory.

Italics within Scripture quotations indicate emphasis added.

All the images in this book are used with permission, Methodist Library Collection, Drew University Library, Madison, New Jersey, USA.

ISBN: 978-1-59638-521-4 (pbk)
ISBN: 978-1-62995-168-3 (ePub)
ISBN: 978-1-62995-169-0 (Mobi)

Page design by Lakeside Design Plus

Printed in the United States of America

Library of Congress Cataloging-in-Publication Data

Schwenk, James L., 1965-
  George Whitefield : a guided tour of his life and thought / James L. Schwenk. -- 1st ed.
      pages cm. -- (The guided tour series)
  Includes bibliographical references and index.
  ISBN 978-1-59638-521-4 (pbk.)
  1. Whitefield, George, 1714-1770. 2. Presbyterian Church--Great Britain--Clergy--Biography. I. Title.
  BX9225.W4S39 2015
  269'.2092--dc23
  [B]
                                        2014048130

For Heather and Tyler

Your mother and I thank God for you every day. It has been our pleasure to introduce you to C. S. Lewis, J. R. R. Tolkien, and *Doctor Who*.

It has been an even greater joy to introduce you to Jesus Christ.

CONTENTS

List of Illustrations   9

Acknowledgments   11

Introduction: Why Read George
Whitefield?   13

**Part One: A Brief Account of the Life of the
Grand Itinerant**

1. The Gloucester Years: The Bell Inn and
   St. Mary de Crypt School   25

2. The Life of God in the Soul of George
   Whitefield: Oxford, Henry Scougal, and
   the Holy Club   33

3. "Look at the Boy Preacher": Closed Pulpits
   and Open Fields   41

4. "It Seemed As If the Whole World Was
   Becoming Religious": Leading Revivals in
   England and North America   55

5. "Catholic Spirit": Controversy and Connections
   Spread the Revivals   71

6. "I Would Rather Wear Out Than Rust Out":
   The Final American Tour   89

Part Two: The Grand Itinerant in Print

7. Excerpts from the Writings of George
   Whitefield   107

   Continuing the Journey: A Brief Guide to
   Works by and about George Whitefield   187

   Bibliography   191

   Index of Subjects and Names   193

ILLUSTRATIONS

3.1   Preaching at Moorfields   45

3.2   Bethesda Orphanage   52

4.1   Unflattering portrait   68

5.1   *Illustrated History of Methodism*   73

5.2   Statue on the campus of the University of
        Pennsylvania   81

6.1   Rosse engraving of George Whitefield   91

6.2   Death repose   99

7.1   Whitefield preaching   139

7.2   Whitefield, older   169

ACKNOWLEDGMENTS

"Friends at first are friends again at last." So wrote the poet Charles Wesley as he reflected on the strained relationship and reunion of his brother, John, and George Whitefield. I have been living with these two friends for the last three decades since I was introduced to them at United Wesleyan College in Allentown, Pennsylvania. As one might expect, Wesley got some pretty good press in a college that bore his name. But while I appreciated Wesley and his role in the Methodist revivals in England and the importation of Methodism to the United States, I was drawn to the man they called the "divine dramatist."

At Evangelical Seminary in Myerstown, Pennsylvania, my church history professor, Dr. Robert Hower, invited me to explore the friendship and strained relationship between Wesley and Whitefield. Later, during my doctoral work at Drew University, I expanded my research on their relationship into my dissertation and my first book, *Catholic Spirit: Wesley, Whitefield, and the Quest for Evangelical Unity in 18th Century British Methodism* (Scarecrow Press, 2008). My friend and colleague, Dr. Leon O. Hynson, a Luther and Wesley scholar, used to tell me, "I like Wesley, but I love Luther." Over the years I have edited Leon's maxim to read, "I like Wesley, but I love Whitefield!" Thank you, Leon and Bob, for encouraging me to pursue a deeper understanding of Whitefield and his message to the world. Thanks are due also to Dr. Ken Rowe, Dr. Chuck Yrigoyen, and Dr. Leigh

Schmidt, all of whom answered many questions, offered sound advice, and sent me in the direction of the materials I needed in order to better know George Whitefield.

I would also like to thank Dr. Steve Nichols of Lancaster Bible College, who invited me to join the LBC family as an adjunct instructor. He learned of my love of Whitefield and invited me to write this book. Thank you for the challenge and for your support throughout the process.

Teachers are nothing without their students. My deepest appreciation goes out to students from University of St. Francis, Messiah College, Evangelical Seminary, Lancaster Theological Seminary, Penn State University (Berks campus), Lancaster Bible College, Lancaster County Christian School, and Zaporozhye Bible College and Seminary (Ukraine) for teaching me, and for challenging me to be a better teacher.

Each week I have the honor of reading God's Word and explaining it to the members and friends of Gingrichs Mennonite Church in Lebanon, Pennsylvania. Thank you for calling me to be your pastor and for being the visible body of Christ in our town and around the world. Your passion for Christ and your patience in allowing me to introduce you to all my "friends" from church history gives me the energy to keep going.

Finally, I want to thank my family for your love, support, prayers, and timely "kicks." Lore, I love you with all my heart and thank God for the first twenty-five years he's given us . . . and I look forward to the next twenty-five! Your love for Jesus is a daily example and encouragement to me. Thank you for loving him as you do. And thank you, Heather and Tyler, for the joy you've brought into our home. This book is dedicated to you.

INTRODUCTION: WHY READ GEORGE WHITEFIELD?

There are few people, dead or alive, for whom I will interrupt a family vacation.

George Whitefield is one of them.

My family has vacationed in North Myrtle Beach, South Carolina, on three occasions. On our second trip, somewhere between the overpriced miniature golf, the afternoons on the beach, and our evening trips to the ubiquitous all-you-can-eat Calabash smorgasbords, I squealed the tires of our Dodge Durango, did a U-turn on the highway, and abruptly stopped along the divided highway. There was a gray-and-white state historical marker with the heading, "George Whitefield."

Two hundred fifty years before our family trip, George Whitefield traveled the Coast Road in Horry County. Just south of Little River, Whitefield, an evangelical priest of the Church of England, stopped at a local tavern to find lodging. These would have been familiar surroundings to Whitefield, who had grown up in the family-owned Bell Inn in Gloucester, England. The date was January 1, 1740. Much like today, the inn was filled with New Year's revelers eating, drinking, and dancing. He wryly noted, "The people were more polite than those we generally met with; but I believe the people of the house wished I had not come to be their guest that night; for, it being New Year's Day, several of the neighbors were met together to divert themselves by dancing country dances."

Encouraged by his traveling companions, Whitefield interrupted a woman dancing a jig. He warned her of "the folly of such entertainments" and tried to "convince her how well pleased the devil was at every step she took." Undaunted, the woman kept dancing; the fiddler played on.

But "there was a new sheriff in town." In drama befitting a John Wayne western, soon the dancer's feet were stilled and the fiddle fell silent by the force of Whitefield's presence and message. But other foes came to the aid of the silenced and prepared to defend their right to "eat, drink, and be merry."

They had met their match. Whitefield narrates victoriously,

> It would have made anyone smile to see how the rest of the company, one by one attacked me, and brought, as they thought, arguments to support their wantonness; but Christ triumphed over Satan. All were soon put to silence, and were, for some time, so overawed, that after I had discoursed with them on the nature of baptism, and the necessity of being born again, in order to enjoy the Kingdom of Heaven, I baptized, at their entreaty, one of their children, and prayed afterwards as I was enabled, and as the circumstances of the company required.

Whitefield and his companions ate a late supper and retired for the night.

And, yes, the fiddler rosined his bow and the dancing resumed. While waiting for sleep to come, Whitefield reflected, "I heard their music and dancing, which made me look back upon my own past follies with shame and confusion of face; for such an one, not long since, was I myself." He prayed,

> Lord, for Thy mercies' sake, shew all unhappy formalists the same favour, and suffer them not to go in such a carnal

security till they lift up their eyes in torment! Draw them, O draw them from feeding upon such husks. Let them know what it is to feast upon the fatted calf, even the comforts of the Blessed Holy Spirit. Amen.

The next day, Whitefield had the last word. "Rose very early, prayed, sang a hymn, and gave a sharp reproof to the dancers, who were very attentive, and took it in good part."

Here were two days' journal entries, the spirit of which was repeated dozens, if not hundreds, of times in the ministry of George Whitefield. He traveled to his next preaching location. He preached the gospel to eager listeners and hecklers alike. He reflected on his own life and how God had prepared him years before, through seemingly insignificant circumstances, for the events of the day. Finally he prayed, giving thanks to God for graciously calling him to be saved and to be one of his messengers, and asking that God might continue to call tavern regulars and innkeepers, fiddlers and dancers, loving parents and their children to become partakers of God's grace.

There are no shortages of biographies of George Whitefield, dating from the eighteenth century to the present. While no recent offerings come close to the exhaustive two-volume classic biography by Arnold Dallimore, contemporary contributions have helped to round out the portrait of Whitefield for the twenty-first century. In his *The Divine Dramatist: George Whitefield and the Rise of Modern Evangelicalism*, Harry Stout reminds readers that Whitefield developed an early love for the stage and employed the principles of effective acting and stage presence each time he took to the pulpit. Whitefield's contributions as a missionary who was heavily invested in the planting of the Georgia colony have been masterfully celebrated by Edward J. Cashin in his work, *Beloved Bethesda: A History of George Whitefield's*

Home for Boys. Jerome Mahaffey claims that Whitefield played a defining role in the birth of the new American republic as a "political preacher" and "accidental revolutionary" (*The Accidental Revolutionary: George Whitefield and the Creation of America*).

This foray into the field of Whitefield biographies is written in honor of the 2014 celebration of the three-hundredth anniversary of Whitefield's birth. Further, it seeks to do what other volumes in the Guided Tour series have accomplished: bring together an accessible biography of a key leader in church history with representative samples of his important contributions to the worship and witness of the church. It recognizes that it is nearly impossible to separate the life story of a Christian leader from the message he or she was called to proclaim. It affirms that the voice of the "Grand Itinerant" needs to be heard today.

As a biography, the first six chapters rediscover Whitefield's life story. Starting with his unassuming beginnings as the son of innkeepers in Gloucester, chapter 1 explores the impact those "blue-collar" surroundings had on young Whitefield. Along with instilling within him a determined work ethic, growing up in the Bell Inn gave Whitefield a deep compassion and concern for the physical and spiritual needs of the working classes. The chapter concludes with an introduction to another formative influence from Whitefield's youth. While a student at St. Mary de Crypt School, Whitefield fell in love—not with learning, but with the stage. His youthful obsession with acting proved providential, as God used that dramatic flair as an important part of Whitefield's powerful gospel proclamations.

Chapter 2 follows Whitefield to Oxford, the city that will provide no fewer than three turning points in his life. Like thousands before and after him, Whitefield studied at Pembroke College, directly across the St. Aldate's Street from the towering edifice of Christ Church. The location proved to be life changing, as Christ Church was the college of John and Charles Wesley. Thousands went to Oxford to study. Few were converted to Christ in the process. Whitefield's conversion, thanks in part to the witness of especially Charles Wesley (and a carefully chosen book), proved to be the most notable conversion at Oxford until the twentieth century, when C. S. Lewis received God's grace after a moonlight stroll along Addison's Walk at Magdalen College with colleagues J. R. R. Tolkien and Hugo Dyson.

Upon his graduation from Oxford, Whitefield sought and received ordination from the Church of England. His ordination to Word and Sacrament, according to the rubrics of the Book of Common Prayer, opened doors for ministry within the established church of his homeland. His message of salvation by grace through faith closed many of those doors as quickly as they opened. The closed pulpits did little to dishearten Whitefield; he simply took the proclamation of the gospel outdoors. His desire to preach where the gospel was not being faithfully proclaimed led him to accept a call to take over from the Wesley brothers as missionary to the fledgling Georgia colony in North America. In Savannah, among the live oaks and Spanish moss, the Wesleys experienced failure and left, never to return to the colonies. Whitefield, however, again fell in love—with Savannah and her citizens, orphans, and slaves—and in the process he began a lifelong relationship with the American colonies that would draw him back six additional times. These are the subjects of chapter 3.

George Whitefield's unique contributions to Christian history include his leadership of revivals in both the British Isles and England's North American colonies. Chapter 4 explores Whitefield's love of his countries: his homeland and his adopted "home." Throughout his ministry, he never forgot about the land of his birth. He was indebted to her for his citizenship and, through the Church of England, his ordination. While often downplaying his connection to the Anglican Church, Whitefield never left, though he was tempted to do so on several occasions—the most notable being Ebenezer and Ralph Erskine's invitation for him to join the Scottish Presbyterians.

Whitefield was torn, however, between his commitments to his homeland and his passion for the fruitful fields of ministry he found in North America. Decades before the American Revolution, Whitefield celebrated the freedom he discovered on the colonial shores: freedom to proclaim the gospel in churches and public settings; freedom to work with like-minded pastors, regardless of denominational label; freedom to express his growing support for the fledgling American calls for independence. Historians from the eighteenth through twenty-first centuries have branded Whitefield "an American patriot," including popular American conservative commentator Glenn Beck, who goes so far as to describe Whitefield as "a rock-star of the Revolution."[1]

Christian leaders of every generation have both attracted controversy and benefited from the power of personal networks of friends and colleagues. George Whitefield was no exception. Whitefield masterfully harnessed the power of America's newspapers and pulpits, and America was blessed with an abundance of both. Pastors and newspaper publishers served as Whitefield's publicists, marketing department, and agents. Major newspapers up and down the East Coast carried announcements of upcoming Whitefield appearances, accounts of his outdoor services, manuscripts of his

1. Glenn Beck, "Founders' Friday: George Whitefield," *Fox News*, May 17, 2010, http://www.foxnews.com/story/2010/05/17/glenn-beck-founders-friday-george-whitefield/.

sermons, and rebuttals by opponents. Through this, Whitefield learned a valuable lesson: both good press and bad
press could help promote a revival. While saying that Whitefield welcomed controversy may be overstatement, to say
that he used controversy to further the spread of the gospel
would not.

Whitefield's use of the press helped him to nurture a
friendship with American printer, philosopher, and statesman, Benjamin Franklin—one of church history's most
unique relationships. While this relationship started as a
business arrangement and led to witnessing opportunities,
another was established on common faith and was tested
in controversy. Whitefield, along with brothers John and
Charles Wesley, shared leadership of the revivals that swept
England during the 1700s. Their friendship deteriorated
as theological differences surfaced that were exacerbated
by supporters both in print and from the pulpit. While
differences never disappeared, Whitefield and the Wesleys
ultimately agreed to spread the gospel according to their
own convictions and to continue to work together as conscience allowed. For them, their common faith and the
importance of sharing God's good news trumped theological differences that their spiritual children continue to
debate today.

A third set of relationships provided an audience for
Whitefield from the upper crust of English society. Thanks
to his friendship with Lady Selina, Countess of Huntington,
Whitefield gained a hearing in the drawing rooms and librar-
ies of some of England's most influential people. While
Whitefield's message never changed, his versatility in tailor-
ing his message to his audience allowed him to be equally
comfortable preaching to Bristol miners or to lords and
ladies. Chapter 5 probes the controversies and connections
that provided hearers for the popular preacher.

The final biographical chapter follows the Grand Itinerant through the final years of his earthly journey. The transatlantic travel and grueling preaching schedule began to take their toll on a man not yet sixty years of age. Traveling to America one final time, Whitefield renewed old friendships and faithfully preached release from sin's bondage to colonists who would soon be fighting for their independence from the British Crown. While he planned on one day being laid to rest in his London Tabernacle between the brothers Wesley, the One who numbers man's days had other plans. In Newburyport, Massachusetts, in September 1770, Whitefield appealed to God that he might "speak for thee once more in the fields, seal thy truth, and come home and die." His request granted, Whitefield was laid to rest in the crypt of the local Presbyterian church, a location that became a site of pilgrimage for many Protestants.

The concluding section of this work contains representative sermons, letters, and journal entries from the hand of George Whitefield. They were chosen to highlight his Reformed theology, his commitment to the preaching of the gospel, his passion for the souls of men and women, and his dedication to principles of freedom.

In 2008 I had the honor of presenting a paper at the C. S. Lewis Foundation's "Oxbridge 2008." An avid fan of "the Inklings," especially of Lewis and J. R. R. Tolkien, I relished the opportunity of visiting the city that was both their home and their academic community. My experience was heightened by the fact that my wife and children were able to accompany me and by the discovery, upon my arrival, that I would be reading my paper at Pembroke College—the school where Tolkien taught and the alma mater of George Whitefield. I find it amusing that two sets of friends—George Whitefield and John Wesley, C. S. Lewis and J. R. R. Tolkien—counted Oxford as an important city to both their academic preparation and to the nurturing of their friendship. The four of them have made an indelible impact on my life. May Whitefield continue to leave such an impact on the lives of those who study his life and ministry and who hear his message thunder down through the centuries.

PART ONE

A Brief Account of the Life of the Grand Itinerant

1

THE GLOUCESTER YEARS: THE BELL INN AND ST. MARY DE CRYPT SCHOOL

Eighteenth-century English mothers did not dream for their children to grow up to be Kingswood coal miners. Work in the mines around Bristol was hard, backbreaking labor. Young boys went into the mines and, if they were fortunate, came out decades later as bent and broken old men. During the 1700s, there was little hope of a Kingswood boy receiving any kind of education that would feed the mind or nourish the soul. Yet coal mining fueled the Kingswood economy since the Middle Ages and continued as such until the last mine closed in the 1950s.

On a February afternoon in 1739, twenty-four-year-old George Whitefield ventured out into the Kingswood coalfields. He was not there looking for a job, nor was he there to lobby for better working conditions for the miners. He had a much deeper concern: the eternal souls of the Kingswood miners. As the miners emerged from their coal pits at the end of the work day, Whitefield, a young Oxford-trained preacher, "went upon a mount, and spoke to as many people as came" to hear him. According to his count, two hundred miners gathered to hear the good news of salvation through Christ. Whitefield became exuberant. "Blessed be God that I have now broken the ice! I believe I never was more acceptable to my Master than when I was standing to teach those hearers in the open fields." After another sermon at the mouth of the mine, Whitefield, filled with emotion, noticed the "miners, just up from the mines, listened and the tears flowed making white gutters down their coal-black faces." It was a dramatic snapshot—one that the young preacher could not miss, and one that would be repeated countless times over the evangelist's thirty-year ministry.

Whitefield, in fact, rarely missed anything dramatic. His sermons were filled with vibrant illustrations drawn from everyday life and from the natural world surrounding him. He has been described as a "divine dramatist," employing stagecraft as he proclaimed God's truth from God's Word. He noticed things that only a trained actor would notice, like white gutters on cheeks stained with coal dust. His movements, his presence, his diction, and his projection all worked together as part of the proclamation of the message that God in his grace had provided a way for lost sinners, even Kingswood miners, to be saved.

Love of the theater was not something Whitefield had developed as an adult. He had developed that passion as a young boy in Gloucester. Many aspiring actors today find waiting tables a necessary occupation while waiting for their "big break." Perhaps Whitefield was the first in a long line of actors just waiting to be discovered, as his first job as a young boy was working in the family inn. God, the Divine Director, had a much more important role for him to play than any he might have played on the London stage.

People in Western cultures love to cheer for the underdog. It may be the team, winless the previous season, who one year later wins the championship. Perhaps it is the city, ravaged by a natural disaster, that rebuilds and restores a booming economy. We cheer for George Bailey, who stands up to Mr. Potter in Frank Capra's classic film *It's a Wonderful Life*, and in the process proves that "Davids" can still defeat even corporate "Goliaths." We embrace those who started life in humble, even difficult, circumstances, and who grow up to succeed far beyond what their beginnings foretold.

This alone attracts students of history to George Whitefield. Born into a still-stratified English society, Whitefield knew nothing of privilege or comfort during his early years. He was born the underdog, but God has a habit of using the foolish, the weak, and the unremarkable to turn the world upside down.

George Whitefield was born into the home of Thomas and Elizabeth Whitefield on December 16, 1714—the same year that Queen Anne died and the Hanoverian, George I, arrived from Germany. The Whitefields owned and operated the Bell Inn located on Southgate Street in Gloucester, England. George was the youngest of seven children Elizabeth bore. Sadly, Thomas died when George was only two years old. Elizabeth remarried, but by all accounts, her second marriage was an unhappy one. Whitefield wrote his reflections on his early years twenty or more years after the fact, so some of the material may not be remembered as accurately as contemporary historians would like it to be. That being said, Whitefield's journals are the best commentary on his early life, as no one else took the time to record it. Who could have imagined the promise that rested deep inside the Bell Inn busboy?

According to Whitefield, someone did get a glimpse of that promise. Elizabeth Whitefield prophesied that "she expected more comfort" from her youngest son than from his older siblings. Whitefield echoed this sentiment, telling the readers of his journals, "I can recollect very early moving of the blessed Spirit upon my heart, sufficient to satisfy me that God loved me with an everlasting love, and separated me even from my mother's womb, for the work to which He afterwards was pleased to call me." Even being born in the Bell Inn fired Whitefield's imagination. It motivated his "endeavors to make good my mother's expectations, and so follow the example of my dear Saviour, who was born in a manger belonging to an inn." Such statements inspired Whitefield and undoubtedly pleased his mother, but they would give his critics ammunition in their attacks on Whitefield as an "Enthusiast"—the eighteenth-century equivalent of being labeled a "Holy Roller."

But Whitefield did not stop there in the vivid description of his early years. Two things stand out in Whitefield's account. First is the description that he gives of himself as a vile sinner. He remembers "such early stirrings of corruption in my heart." He catalogues the sins of his childhood, including lying, filthy talking, foolish jesting, cursing, swearing, and stealing. Growing up in the public house atmosphere, he not surprisingly picked up some of the "local dialect." He broke the Sabbath and behaved "very irreverently in God's sanctuary." Stealing from his mother, he sometimes bought food to satisfy his "sensual appetite." Occasionally he bought plays to read—the most alluring of his boyhood temptations. He played cards, read romances, and played practical jokes. Readers get the sense that they are back in North Africa with young Augustine as Whitefield records among his early sins the theft of his neighbor's pears. Whitefield is disturbed, and rightly so, by the catalogue of sins he records. But the listing serves to remind him of the overwhelming free grace of God, which he understood was an undeserved gift.

Whatever foreseen fitness for salvation others may talk of and glory in, I disclaim any such thing. If I trace myself from my cradle to my manhood, I can see nothing in me but a fitness to be damned. . . . If the Almighty had not prevented me by His grace, and wrought most powerfully upon my soul, quickening me by His free Spirit when dead in trespasses and sins, I had now either been sitting in darkness, and in the shadow of death, or condemned, as the due reward of my crimes, to be forever lifting up my eyes in torments.

The second thing that stands out in Whitefield's account of his childhood is the account's brevity. Whitefield provides few details for his readers. He covers his entire life from birth to his going up to Oxford in ten pages of a five-hundred-page document. Perhaps he is again modeling the account of his early years on the gospel accounts of Jesus' life, which highlight his birth and a cameo appearance when he is an adolescent. Perhaps this is because the growing-up years of both men were so very much like those of their contemporaries.

The Gloucester in which Elizabeth Whitefield raised her children may not have been as important a city as Oxford or London to the English-speaking Christian world, but neither was it an insignificant footnote. Its founding is shrouded in the mists of pre-Roman Britain. Its Christian heritage dates back at least to the seventh century, when Osric, King of Hwicce, founded the monastery of St. Peter, which would become the foundation of the Gloucester Cathedral. Rebuilt after a fire in 1088, the new, yet-to-be-completed cathedral was dedicated in 1100. If the walls of Gloucester Cathedral could talk, the stones would bear witness to the murder of King Edward II, who is buried in its crypt. They would speak of visits by Richard II, Henry VII, and even Henry VIII. And they would recount the burning of Bishop John Hooper, reformer of Gloucester, who died at the behest of Queen Mary. And now, nearly two hundred years later, Elizabeth Whitefield was raising a new reformer who would wear the mantle passed on by the heroic Hooper.

The city of Gloucester has entertained royal visits and sessions of Parliament. During the English Civil War, it sided with Parliament and defied the rule of Charles I. Now, each Christmas, the city sends a gift of an eel pie to the monarch as a symbol of its loyalty to the Crown.

Gloucester cathedral stood as a symbol of Christianity's enduring legacy in the city. But it was a much smaller church where young George Whitefield received his early Christian nurture. He was baptized as an infant at a font that still stands in the St. Mary de Crypt Church on Southgate Street. One of only twelve medieval English churches with a crypt, St. Mary's is first mentioned in twelfth-century annals, and it went through major reconstruction in the late fourteenth century, with further remodeling accomplished through the next two centuries. During the siege of Gloucester in 1643, the church served as an ammunition factory and magazine— a bit of its martial history preserved in chevrons and cannonballs baked into some of the tiles in the choir.

The crypt of St. Mary's holds the earthly remains of several notable people. Robert Raikes, who founded the Sunday school movement in the Old Crypt Schoolroom, is buried under the floor of the South Chapel. Jemmy Wood is also buried at St. Mary's. Wood, a notorious, miserly banker, reportedly scoured the docks of Gloucester for wayward pieces of coal so he would have to purchase less. Once he traveled home to Gloucester in the back of an empty hearse so he would not have to pay carriage fare. His penny-pinching reputation reached the ears of Charles Dickens, who reportedly immortalized Wood as literature's most famous miser, Ebenezer Scrooge.

The Whitefield family worshiped at St. Mary's, and young George received his early education in the grammar school connected to the church. The school, founded in 1539, provided Whitefield with the basic educational skills that would serve him throughout his lifetime. Here again, Whitefield's

training would have been no different from any of his contemporaries who attended a grammar school attached to a
local parish church. The study of Greek and Latin and of
the classics of Greek and Rome were staples of the eighteenth-century educational diet, and any young man expect-
ing to pursue higher education would be expected to master
these elements of the curriculum. Young Whitefield does
not distinguish himself as a scholar at St. Mary's. He does,
however, attract the attention of the schoolmaster with his
acting ability. At times he stayed away from school for days
so he could devote the bulk of his time to memorizing lines
for an upcoming school performance. Recognizing his tal-
ent, Whitefield's schoolmaster wrote a play and cast George
in a female role. Of having to dress as a woman and play the
part, Whitefield admitted it "covered me with confusion of
face, and I hope will do so, even to the end of my life."

Poor grades, no clear future direction for his life, no moti-
vation to pursue university studies, and the necessity of helping to keep the family business afloat encouraged fifteen-
year-old George to leave school. He worked in the Bell Inn
even after his mother passed it on to one of his older brothers.
A disagreement with his sister-in-law led him to leave Gloucester to settle with another brother in Bristol. Two months later
he was back in his hometown, living with his mother and
actively seeking an apprenticeship. No doors opened for him.
At this point in his life, with no apparent direction on the
horizon, Whitefield details another prophecy he privately
shared with his sister: "God intends something for me which
we know not of. As I have been diligent in business, I believe
many would gladly have me for an apprentice, but every way
seems to be barred up, so that I think God will provide for
me some way or other that we cannot apprehend."

God's provision of "a way" came through the visit of a
former classmate of Whitefield. The visitor was a student

at Pembroke College, Oxford, where he paid for his education as a servitor to wealthier students. This position can be likened to today's work-study programs. Servitors cooked, cleaned, and did menial tasks for wealthy students who understood such work as beneath their social status. Whitefield's former classmate reported that by working as a servitor, he had paid all his expenses the previous quarter, with a whole penny left over! The news convinced Elizabeth that this was the way her son could attend Oxford and perhaps fulfill the premonition of great things in store for George she had had at his birth. George agreed with her conclusion. His years of on-the-job training, waiting tables in the family inn, prepared him well for life as an Oxford servitor.

Now that he had caught a glimpse of where his future might lead, George returned to school in Gloucester to better prepare for the academic rigors of university life. He went up to Oxford in November 1732, enrolling as a student in Pembroke College, a school located behind St. Aldate's Church, directly across St. Aldate's Street from Christ Church College and Cathedral—a piece of geographic serendipity that would play a meaningful part in Whitefield's spiritual journey.

At Pembroke, the former server at the Bell Inn served wealthy students as a means to pay for his education. The work was hard, not only physically but emotionally, as the social stratification of England encouraged the students from the upper crust to look down upon those, like Whitefield, from the merchant class. When his work serving other students was done, Whitefield still had to attend to his own studies. Disconnected from family and home, subjected to the whims of his social superiors, and facing the pressures of keeping up with his own studies, Whitefield sought solace in the faith planted in him in his youth at St. Mary's in Gloucester. Those seeds, planted years before, would soon bear fruit as George Whitefield met Charles Wesley.

2

THE LIFE OF GOD IN THE SOUL
OF GEORGE WHITEFIELD:
OXFORD, HENRY SCOUGAL,
AND THE HOLY CLUB

If George Whitefield could visit Oxford today, some of what he discovered would boggle his mind. Yet after coming to grips with modern transportation and wireless communication, our visitor from the eighteenth century would find much of today's Oxford familiar. The names of most of the colleges and halls of the university would remind Whitefield of his days there. Many of the volumes in the Bodleian Library today were accessible to Whitefield and his fellow students. Descendants of the red deer of Magdalene College still roam the fields along the River Charwell.

Also familiar would be the atmosphere that makes the nurturing of one's faith challenging in such an academic setting. The scientific and philosophical debates in Whitefield's Oxford might not have risen to the heights of those of twenty-first-century Oxford between Richard Dawkins and John Lennox. But the thought life of eighteenth-century Oxford was being impacted by the early stages of the Enlightenment, through which traditional understandings of the world and the universe were being called into question. Tutors were expected to read and were required to affirm their adherence to the Thirty-Nine Articles of Religion of the Church of England, but no less a commentator than Edmund Gibbon quipped that the Articles were "signed by more than read, and read by more than believe them." The "gleaming spires" of Oxford hid a generation of professors whose days were filled with making the rounds of "the chapel, the hall, the coffee house, and the common room," until they ended their day with a long, peaceful slumber. Gibbon suggested that, "from the tasks of reading, and thinking or writing, they had absolved their consciences."

One must always be careful of taking one man's opinion too seriously when addressing a situation of which he was part. And, no doubt, there were those who were as positive of their assessment of the Oxford of Whitefield's day as Gibbon was negative in his. The case was serious enough in the minds of the university's administration that the vice-chancellor stepped in to remedy what he saw as not just an academic issue but a spiritual matter as well. He posted a notice informing all tutors of their Christian duty, chief of which was their responsibility not just to know and accept the Articles of Religion, but to teach them to the students in their charge. Further, the vice-chancellor recommended the frequent, careful reading of Scripture, "and other books that may serve more effectually to promote Christianity, sound principles, and orthodox faith." At least one tutor took the directive seriously. Charles Wesley recorded, "Diligence led me into serious thinking. I went to the weekly Sacrament, and persuaded two or three young scholars to accompany me, and to observe the method of study prescribed by the Statutes of the University." He adds, almost as an afterthought, "This gained me the harmless nickname of a Methodist."

Meanwhile, Whitefield had matriculated to Pembroke College, Oxford. Like many young college students, Whitefield received invitations to "join in the excesses" of his roommates, but he reports victoriously that, "God, in answer to prayers before put up, gave me grace to withstand them; and once in particular, it being cold, my limbs were so benumbed by sitting alone in my study, because I would not go out amongst them, that I could scarce sleep all night." Soon enough, those who urged him to join in their collegiate pranks stopped inviting him, concluding that he was "a singular odd fellow." This is not to suggest that Whitefield had left all of his old temptations behind him, for he admits to playing an occasional game of cards and to reading a play from time to time. But even then God laid conviction upon his heart, and he soon left the decks of cards and books of plays in the dust.

Along with leaving certain practices behind him, Whitefield also started practicing positive spiritual disciplines while at Oxford. "I now began to pray and sing psalms thrice every day, besides morning and evening, and to fast every Friday, and to receive the Sacrament at a parish church near our college, and at the castle, where the despised Methodists used to receive once a month." The Methodists, members of the so-called "Holy Club" begun by Charles Wesley and later joined by his older brother John, were becoming known in and around Oxford as quite a religious oddity. Whitefield was attracted to their commitment to living "by rule and method." For over a year he watched the Methodists from afar, not having the courage to join their number, even though strongly impressed by their boldly marching to St. Mary's Cathedral, through a ridiculing crowd, to receive the Eucharist.

It was a tragic event that brought George Whitefield and Charles Wesley together. A poverty-stricken woman attempted suicide in one of the local workhouses. Whitefield, knowing of the Wesleys' commitment to works of mercy in the community, sent word to Charles asking him to help in whatever way he could. Contrary to Whitefield's wishes, his messenger revealed to Wesley that Whitefield had requested his assistance, and as a result, Charles invited Whitefield to breakfast the next morning. His reluctance at being revealed as the originator of the message now gone, Whitefield writes, "I thankfully embraced the opportunity; and, blessed be God! it was one of the most profitable visits I ever made in my life. My soul, at that time, was athirst for some spiritual friends to lift up my hands when they hung down, and to strengthen my feeble knees." Charles recognized Whitefield as a seeker after true faith and became his spiritual guide, mentor, and chief provider of reading material.

Whitefield's reading list never reached the length of the Wesley brothers', particularly John's. But what he lacked in breadth, he made up for in depth. A rapid scan of his *Journals* and *Letters* reveals theological and devotional works that had already impacted generations of readers and newer volumes that were now sculpting the spiritual development of interested readers in Whitefield's day. This collection of books shaped Whitefield, beginning even before arriving at Oxford, and continuing throughout his ministry.

His list of spiritual guides is impressive. Thomas á Kempis became an early and regular mentor, as Whitefield was introduced to his *Imitation of Christ* while staying with his brother in Bristol as an adolescent. English mystic William Law received high praise from Whitefield. He knew of Law's *Serious Call to a Devout and Holy Life* prior to going up to Oxford but could not afford his own copy. When finally able to read it at university, Whitefield proclaimed, "God worked powerfully upon my soul, as He has since upon many others, by that and his other excellent treatise upon *Christian Perfection*."

Whitefield gratefully remembered Charles Wesley as one who introduced him to numerous spiritual directors. Wesley gave Whitefield *Against the Fear of Man*, authored by German Pietist August Hermann Franke. If the book itself did not impact Whitefield, the example of Franke's life did, as Whitefield patterned much of his ministry to orphans, prisoners, and the poor on the work of the German Pietiest from Halle.

Charles Wesley also lent Whitefield *The Country Parson's Advice to His Parishioners*. The anonymously authored book, published in 1680, was subtitled, "A Serious Exhortation to a Religious and Virtuous Life." The author set out to give "the best assistance [I] can in a religious and virtuous life; to direct you how to live to God's glory, and to attain that perfect and happy estate which God has made you capable of, and which your Saviour desires to bring you to, by that holy religion which you profess." Whitefield praised it as a book that "was wonderfully blessed to my soul."

Hidden in this list of books instrumental to his spiritual development is one work Whitefield accorded special honor. He read it during his Oxford years, and it was integral to his conversion while he was a student at Pembroke College. Charles Wesley was again responsible for the introduction. "In a short time," Whitefield notes, "he let me have another book, entitled *The Life of God in the Soul of Man*." Written by Scottish Presbyterian Henry Scougal, *The Life of God* was first published in 1677 as a letter of spiritual direction to a friend. Scougal was raised in the home of a Presbyterian minister whose library was filled with books written by Pietists and Christian mystics. As a result of reading through his father's library, Scougal concluded that religious formalism and sectarian strife had taken the place of vital, inward faith. In writing *The Life of God*, Scougal sought "to inspire us with the spirit of true religion, to enlighten our minds with a right sense and knowledge of it, to warm our hearts with suitable affections and breathings after it, and to direct our lives to the practice of it." The work had its intended effect on George Whitefield.

At first, Scougal's premise confused Whitefield. In *The Life of God* he argues that many people make mistakes concerning the nature of true religion. "Some place it in the understanding—in orthodox notions and opinions . . . others place it in the affections—in rapturous heats and ecstatic devotion." Still others think true religion consists "in a constant course of external duties," like living at peace with one's neighbors, keeping a temperate diet, regularly attending worship, keeping times of public and private prayer, and giving to the relief of the poor. After reading this, Whitefield wondered, "If this be not true religion, what is?" He did not have to read much farther. Scougal explained, "True religion is a union of the soul with God, a real participation of the divine nature, the very image of God drawn upon the soul; or in the apostle's phrase, it is Christ formed within us. Briefly, I know not how the nature of religion can be more fully expressed, than by calling it a divine life." Now, with new enlightenment, Whitefield exclaims, "A ray of Divine light was instantaneously darted in upon my soul, and from that moment, but not till then, did I know that I must be a new creature."

While the burst of "Divine light" may well have been instantaneous, Whitefield's surrender to Jesus Christ would take some time. He continued to attend meetings of the Holy Club and willingly received instruction from Charles Wesley. Further, he adopted the "living by rule" practiced by the Methodists: redeeming every minute of the day, fasting on Wednesdays and Fridays, attending the weekly Sacrament, visiting the sick and imprisoned. He modified his reading to include "books that entered into the heart of religion, and which led . . . directly into an experimental knowledge of

Jesus Christ, and him crucified," leaving behind "the dry sciences and books that went no farther than the surface." His new lifestyle attracted the negative attention of both family and fellow Oxonians. He had fallen into a dangerous outward appearance of humility and sanctity that Scougal warned against and which Charles Wesley was not prepared to counter. He suggested that Whitefield needed to consult his older brother John as one "more experienced" in the spiritual life. It was the beginning of a friendship that would last a lifetime, even though it would be tried by fire.

Whitefield practiced such rigorous fasting during Lent of 1735 that it nearly broke his health completely, resulting in his tutor sending a doctor to treat him. During a two-month recuperation, Whitefield prayed and read the Scriptures and devotional literature as his strength allowed. He records his spiritual victory in biblical metaphors.

> One day, perceiving an uncommon drought and a disagreeable clamminess in my mouth and using things to allay my thirst, but in vain, it was suggested to me, that when Jesus Christ cried out, "I thirst," His sufferings were near at an end. Upon which I cast myself down on the bed, crying out, "I thirst! I thirst!" Soon after this, I found and felt in myself that I was delivered from the burden that had so heavily oppressed me. The spirit of mourning was taken from me, and I knew what it was truly to rejoice in God my Saviour; and, for some time, could not avoid singing psalms wherever I was; but my joy gradually became more settled, and, blessed be God, has abode and increased in my soul, saving a few casual intermissions, ever since. Thus were the days of my mourning ended. . . . Now did the Spirit of God take possession of my soul.

Whitefield took the occasion of his conversion as an opportunity to return home to Gloucester and share his newly found faith with family and friends. Some were excited about the change they saw in their hometown boy; others were skeptical about the new birth he now proclaimed. After a nine-month leave of absence from university, Whitefield returned pondering his future vocation. From the time he entered Oxford, he considered the possibility of preparing for ordination within the Church of England, but now, as he returned to the City of Gleaming Spires, he "entertained high thoughts of the importance of the ministerial office, and was not solicitous what place should be prepared for me, but how I should be prepared for the place." His own uncertainty was increased by the various counselors he consulted—some who encouraged his entrance into the ministry, others who tried to dissuade him. A timely invitation to visit Bishop Benson of Gloucester, and the assurance from him that he would ordain Whitefield whenever he decided to receive holy orders, convinced Whitefield that God was indeed calling him and preparing the way for him to become a priest of the Church of England. The only question that remained was where he would serve.

Bishop Benson considered stationing Whitefield at two small parishes within his jurisdiction. But Sir John Philips, a strong supporter of the group of Methodists at Oxford and later a member of the Fetter Lane Society, promised Whitefield an annual stipend of £30 if he committed to stay at Oxford and oversee the work of the Holy Club, as the Wesleys had left the previous year for missionary work in the North American colony of Georgia. Realizing that caring for the sick and visiting the prisoners would be all a young priest could handle, Whitefield contented himself with remaining at Oxford after receiving his bachelor's degree from Pembroke College. Before his twenty-second birthday, Whitefield had moved from "a servitor to a Bachelor of Arts" and "from a common drawer to a clergyman." Soon the "boy preacher" would debut in both the national and international pulpits.

3

"LOOK AT THE BOY PREACHER": CLOSED PULPITS AND OPEN FIELDS

The history of Christianity in England is shrouded in the mists of both ancient history and legend. While the true history of the church's establishment in the British Isles may lack the romance of the legendary account of its planting by Joseph of Arimathea, as on the continent, it is an account of the trial, tragedy, and ultimate triumph of the gospel. The coming of the Protestant Reformation in the mid-sixteenth century and the subsequent birth of the Church of England assured England of a Protestant future rooted firmly in its Roman Catholic past. Since Queen Elizabeth I oversaw the creation of the *via media*, the "middle way" between Roman Catholicism and Genevan Protestantism, England had been part of the Protestant world—though it was Protestant with a Catholic twist. There had been flirtations with Roman Catholicism during the reign of Charles I and the brief reign of James II, which was cut short by the Glorious Revolution of 1688 that brought Protestants William and Mary to the throne. The religious pendulum had even swung toward the Reformed wing of the Reformation during the English Civil War of the mid-seventeenth century. By Whitefield's day, the Church of

England was the firmly established faith of the land, with a strong Dissenting tradition represented both on the island and in her North American colonies.

Whitefield took seriously his preparation for his ordination. The Church of England of his day had a two-step ordination process: One would be ordained first as a deacon. Then, after further experience in ministry, he could proceed to be fully ordained as a priest. The candidate for orders spent days in the study of the Scriptures that addressed the qualifications for ministry. Whitefield studied the Thirty-Nine Articles of Religion of the Church of England, proving them through scriptural arguments. He fasted, prayed, and spent time in seclusion. On Trinity Sunday 1736 in Gloucester Cathedral, Bishop Benson laid his hands on Whitefield's head and welcomed him into the first step of holy orders. Of that moment, Whitefield remarked, "I offered up my whole spirit, soul and body, to the service of God's sanctuary." The next Sunday he preached his first sermon as an ordained clergyman in St. Mary de Crypt Church, the church of his childhood. He titled it, "The Necessity and Benefit of Religious Society."

Whitefield took as his text Ecclesiastes 4:9–12, which reads in part, "Two are better than one; because they have a good reward for their labour." The "sad decay of true Christianity," argues Whitefield, can be linked to the unwillingness of many Christians to unite themselves into mutually encouraging religious societies. Christians today might call them "small groups." He begins by proving from Scripture the verity of the statement, "Two are better than one." In his second point he gives reasons why such is the case, including helping a fallen friend to his feet, keeping each other warm, and defending one another when attacked. The young preacher masterfully applies these points to his hearers' situation, showing them "the several duties incumbent on every member of a religious society"; namely, mutual reproof, exhortation, assistance, and defending each other. He concludes by encouraging his hearers "to go on in the way you have begun, and by constant, conscientious attendance on your respective societies, to discountenance vice, encourage virtue, and build each other up in the knowledge and fear of God."

In a letter to a friend written later the next week, Whitefield pondered his own assessment of his first public sermon and anecdotal evidence from his listeners. "I trust I was enabled to speak with some degree of authority," he penned. "Some few mocked, but most for the present seemed struck; and I have since heard, that a complaint had been made to the bishop, that I drove fifteen mad the first sermon. The worthy prelate, as I am informed, wished that the madness might not be forgotten before next Sunday."

Whitefield soon returned to Oxford, initially planning on picking up the leadership of the Methodists still living there and in taking an advanced degree. But as more preaching opportunities came his way, Whitefield discovered a new love in proclaiming the gospel truth, which had its roots in his childhood love of the stage. Soon an invitation came from a priest in London for Whitefield to take charge of his parish while the priest was out of town. It was the first "road trip" for the future itinerant evangelist.

Preaching in the capital city could have provided opportunity for pride to grow in the young Whitefield. Fortunately, God, in his rich mercy, has a way of using other people to keep the feet of the potentially prideful squarely on the ground. Whitefield wrote of the shopkeepers who stood in their doorways to see such a young man pass wearing his clerical vestments. One woman remarked, "There's a boy parson." Of her exclamation, Whitefield commented that it "served to mortify my pride." His interim pastoral duties kept him in London for two months in the late summer of 1736.

It is important to note that during the early years of his ministry, Whitefield preached almost exclusively in local parish churches of the Church of England at the invitation of the parish priests. He had been ordained to the first stage of Anglican ordination and was fully committed to the doctrines, rites, and rules of the established church. He cherished the Thirty-Nine Articles of Religion, the Church of England liturgy, and the Book of Common Prayer. Whitefield never separated himself from the Church of England and would have been content to preach exclusively in the pulpits of local churches. The time would come, however, when many pulpits of his own denomination were closed to him. But he would find the pulpits of other denominations swinging wide open to welcome him, and he would find his largest audiences under the open skies.

Whitefield records the first instance of pulpits closed to him by fellow clergymen in the fall of 1737. As his popularity spread through London, several pastors lodged complaints that Whitefield was becoming too popular. Visitors from the community crowded out parishioners. Crowds ruined the church pews. A rumor circulated that the bishop of London intended to censure and silence Whitefield. A visit to the bishop proved the rumor false, but some fellow preachers took their own steps to silence Whitefield. "Two clergymen sent for me," Whitefield recorded, "and told me they would not let me preach in their pulpits any more, unless I renounced that part of my sermon on regeneration, wherein I wished, 'that my brethren would entertain their auditories oftener with discourses upon the new birth.' This I had no freedom to do, and so they continued my opposers." Others opposed Whitefield on the basis of his cordial relationships with Dissenting pastors who fully agreed with him regarding the doctrine of the new birth. The preaching of this doctrine had fallen on hard times in the Church of England. Whitefield supported its recapture. The Dissenters found in him a kindred spirit.

3.1 Preaching at Moorfields. Whitefield preached wherever he could gather an audience.

Already at this early stage of his ministry, Whitefield exhibited his willingness to preach the good news wherever the doors opened to him. Gloucester, Oxford, and London all provided ready-made audiences for him. Invitations poured in for Whitefield to preach throughout England, including one of her faraway colonies. It proved an invitation Whitefield could not refuse, and it benefited British interests and the kingdom of God on both sides of "the Pond."

England's North American colonies exhibited characteristics of the Christian communities who settled in them. Puritanism reigned in much of New England. Pennsylvania, William Penn's "Holy Experiment," welcomed adherents to faiths across the religious spectrum, including Quakers,

Lutherans, Pietists, Catholics, Anglicans, and Anabaptists. Anglicanism flourished in Virginia and fared well in other southern locations like Charleston, South Carolina. Separating South Carolina from Spanish Florida was land soon to be settled by England that would bear the name of the current monarch and be christened Georgia. Since this was a colony settled under the authority of the Crown, it is not surprising that the clearest reflection of Christianity in Georgia would be the established Church of England. Invitations went out for missionaries willing to risk the perilous sea voyage to the New World and to attempt the planting of the Anglican Church among a population of adventurers and prisoners. Members of the Oxford Holy Club answered the call.

John and Charles Wesley responded first. Neither of them was spiritually or emotionally prepared for the missionary lifestyle. John returned to England with a broken heart and a broken spirit. "I went to America to convert Indians," he nobly confessed, "but who will convert me?" He left America never to return. Prior to his return trip, John wrote to Whitefield, speaking of the fields of Georgia that were ripe for the gospel harvest. All that was needed were laborers. The question he aimed at Whitefield was simply, "What if thou art the man?" When John returned to England with his tail between his legs, his tune had changed. Whitefield, already on board the ship *Whitaker* outbound for Georgia, received a message from the inbound Wesley. Wesley had cast a lot—a method he used from time to time to help determine God's will in a given situation. According to Wesley's interpretation of the lot, God wanted Whitefield to turn around and stay in England. Whitefield understood God's will for him to be very different. He left his homeland and arrived in Savannah, Georgia, on May 7, 1738. He wrote in his journal for the date, "Arrived at Savannah Town about seven this evening. . . . How sweetly does Providence order things for us? Oh may I constantly follow it as the Wise Men did the star in the East." Whitefield followed Providence to America seven times. Wesley left America in disgrace, never to return. Whitefield soon discovered he could not stay away.

The Georgia settlers and colonial trustees laid out big plans for their new pastor. "It was resolved that I should have a house and tabernacle built at Frederica, and serve at Savannah, when, and as long as, I pleased." Perhaps realizing the turbulence left in the wake of Wesley's leaving, Whitefield continued, "I find there are many divisions amongst the inhabitants; but God, I hope, will make me an instrument of composing them. Grant this, O Lord, for thy dear Son's sake!" But when he mentions his friend by name, he has nothing but praise for the work he accomplished while in Georgia. "The good, Mr. John Wesley has done in America, under God, is inexpressible. . . . Oh, that I may follow him, and he has Christ."

If the trustees and settlers had big plans for Whitefield in Georgia, his own plans eclipsed theirs in size and scope. As he got to know his people and his parish, he quickly recognized that the needs of the colony were pressing. The children of the colony, especially the underprivileged and orphans, had no opportunity for basic education or learning a trade. Whitefield seized the opportunity to follow the example of August Hermann Franke and the Pietists of Halle, Germany. A century earlier, the Halle Pietists had built the largest orphan house in the world. Whitefield sought to replicate it on a smaller scale in the New World. If God would only "stir up the wills of His faithful people" to fund such an enterprise, Whitefield could easily erect an orphan house at Savannah. Its establishment would have to await a later trip to America, but it would prove to be a legacy that continues to thrive almost three centuries later.

As he left Georgia, Whitefield's passion for his new "home" is evident.

> My heart was full, and I took the first opportunity of venting it by prayer and tears. I think I never parted from a place with more regret; for America in my opinion is an excellent school to learn Christ in, and I have great hopes some good will come out of Savannah because the longer I continued there, the larger the congregations grew. And I scarce knew a night, though we had divine service twice a day, when the Church House has not been nearly full—a proof, this, I hope, that God has yet spiritual and temporal blessings in store for them. Hasten, O Lord, that blessed time!

God had great things in store for America, and Whitefield would be back to participate in them.

For the moment, Whitefield was content to return to England to take the next step in his ordination process. On January 14, 1739, he was ordained a priest of the Church of England in Oxford. He celebrated the day by doing what he loved best: preaching no less than three times to crowded congregations.

Whitefield continued to preach wherever he could find an audience. The proclamation of the gospel was always his primary goal, but as evidenced by his journal entries, Georgia was always on his mind. He began to receive donations for the proposed orphan house, often commenting that a large portion of the offering consisted of coins of the smallest denomination, suggesting that even the poor were moved to give even as they struggled to survive.

His popularity and audiences growing, a strange yet exciting idea came to Whitefield. On January 21, 1739, he preached in a church in London to a "standing room only" crowd. The overflow crowd in the churchyard was estimated at "near a thousand." By Whitefield's accounting, "hundreds more returned home that could not come in." According to a note added to the 1756 edition of his journals, he stated, "This put me first upon thinking of preaching without doors [i.e., outside]. I mentioned it to some friends, who looked upon it as a mad notion. However we kneeled down and prayed that nothing may be done rashly." Sometimes genius lies hidden in the maddest ideas.

Several forces worked in concert to drive Whitefield to adopt field preaching as his primary vehicle for preaching the gospel. One of the forces was crowd size. Small parish churches could not hold the audiences Whitefield attracted. At Basingstoke in February 1739, he perceived that interest in hearing the Word explained was high, so short-notice invitations were sent out and Whitefield preached in the largest room he could find: the dining room of the local inn. "Blessed be God for this opportunity!" he wrote. "I hope I shall learn more and more every day, that no place is amiss for preaching the Gospel." Taking the gospel outdoors could not be far behind. In the very next sentence, Whitefield underscores the second reason for taking his preaching outdoors.

> God forbid, that the Word of God should be bound, because some out of a misguided zeal deny the use of their churches. Though they bid me to no more speak to the people in this way, yet I cannot but speak the things that I have seen and felt in my own soul. The more I am bidden to hold my peace, the more earnestly will I lift up my voice like a trumpet, and tell the people what must be done in them before they can be finally saved by Jesus Christ.

Practicality coupled with a passion for God and for people's eternal well-being drove Whitefield to preach in the fields.

Priests continued to close pulpits to Whitefield, so slowly but surely he overcame what prejudices to field preaching he still harbored. In mid-February, Whitefield started a preaching tour of the Bristol area. Facing some opposition from a local priest, he turned his attention to audiences often neglected by the local clergy. In regular visits to Newgate prison, Whitefield preached the gospel and led worship for the prison population.

Soon he learned of another neglected audience: the coal miners of Kingswood. His heart broke for them. "My bowels have long yearned toward the poor colliers, who are very numerous, and as sheep having no shepherd." They might not come to him, but he would surely go to them, even if it meant preaching to them as they left the mines. After dinner on Saturday, February 17, he "went upon a mount, and spoke to as many people as came unto me. They were upwards of two hundred. Blessed be God that I have now broken the ice!" He sensed the divine approval accompanying his decision. "I believe I never was more acceptable to my Master than when I was standing to teach those hearers in the open fields. Some may censure me, but if I thus pleased men, I should not be the servant of Christ." In less than a week, his coal miner congregation swelled to two thousand, then ten thousand. "The fire is kindled in the country," Whitefield celebrated, "and I know, all the devils of hell shall not be able to quench it."

By March, field preaching had become standard operating procedure for Whitefield. "My preaching in the fields may displease some timorous, bigoted men, but I am thoroughly persuaded it pleases God, and why should I fear anything else?" The proof of its effectiveness was in the crowds: "Blessed be God, all things happen for the furtherance of the Gospel. I now preach to ten times more people than I should, if I had been confined to the churches." And, after all, he had a biblical mandate. He was reminded of Jesus' command to "Go out into the highways and hedges, and compel them to come in." To those who accused him of willfully choosing the novelty of field preaching over preaching inside church buildings, Whitefield countered, "Let not the adversaries say, I have thrust myself out of their synagogues. No; they have thrust me out."

With Georgia never far from his thoughts, Whitefield met with the trustees of the colony in May 1739. They granted him five hundred acres of land on which to establish his longed-for orphan house. He continued to take regular collections for the orphanage and booked passage on the ship *Elizabeth* to return to America as soon as she sailed. After a long delay, the ship set sail in August, arriving in Philadelphia two months later. There Whitefield picked up where he left off in England, preaching outdoors. He preached from the stairs of the courthouse in Philadelphia and surmised that, unlike England, "where the generality of people think a sermon cannot be preached well without, here, they do not like it so well if delivered within the church walls." And as in England, many Church of England pulpits, like the one in Elizabethtown, New Jersey, were closed to him. But while some pulpits slammed shut, others were opened, as American Dissenters found in Whitefield a kindred spirit.

Still other doors opened in Whitefield's path. In January 1740, Whitefield arrived in Georgia and began one of the defining and lasting contributions of his life's work. "Went . . . and took possession of my lot. I called it Bethesda, that is, the House of Mercy; for I hope many acts of mercy will be shewn there, and that many will thereby be stirred up to praise the Lord, as a God Whose mercy endureth for ever." The first of many underprivileged children whose lives would be forever changed at Bethesda moved in the following week. The first stones of the foundation of the main house were laid and dedicated by Whitefield in March.

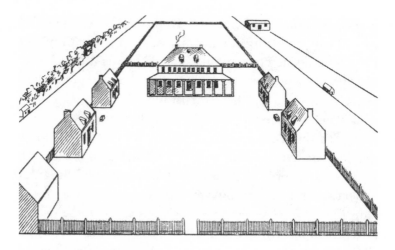

3.2 Founded by Whitefield in 1740, the Bethesda Orphanage (now Bethesda Academy) continues to operate on its founding principles of love for God, love for learning, and a strong work ethic.

The positive impact of Bethesda on young lives is over-shadowed by an unfortunate specter in Whitefield's life. While his friend John Wesley became an outspoken critic of slavery and an encourager of the abolition movement in England, George Whitefield became a slave owner. He deemed them essential to the success of Bethesda. He tried to rationalize it by arguing that countries with hot climates needed the strength and endurance of the slaves. While stating that the slave trade should "not be approved of," he argued that it would continue regardless of his stance on the issue. Furthermore, he would make the lives of any slaves he purchased "comfortable, and lay a foundation for breeding up their posterity in the nurture and admonition of the Lord." It is disappointing that while recognizing the importance of educating and evangelizing slaves, he continued to help propagate the system of slavery that would later tear apart America's fabric of liberty. He planned on establishing a "negro school" in southeastern Pennsylvania, actually purchasing the land and christening it Nazareth (which was appropriate as it was situated just north of the Moravian settlement known as Bethlehem). It never took root. Whitefield abandoned the project, turned it over to the Moravians, and concentrated his energies on Bethesda. Still, Whitefield desired to see African-Americans in God's kingdom. "I doubt not, when the poor negroes are to be called, God will highly favour them, to wipe off their reproach, and show that He is no respecter of persons, but that whoever believeth in Him shall be saved." God could be counted on to free them from bondage; sadly, George Whitefield could not.

As he prepared to leave Savannah in June 1740, he spoke of his deepening love for his "home" in North America. "I believe Savannah will yet become the joy of the earth." High praise for a new city in a backwoods corner of the British Empire! Whitefield's attention for a time was drawn north, and as it was, the way was being paved for him to play a leading role in revivals that would sweep not only North America, but through the British Isles as well.

4

"IT SEEMED AS IF THE WHOLE WORLD WAS BECOMING RELIGIOUS": LEADING REVIVALS IN ENGLAND AND NORTH AMERICA

Thomas Jefferson. John Adams. James Madison. Thomas Paine. George Washington. Benjamin Franklin. North America of the eighteenth century was a greenhouse of political theorists and practitioners. These names would become synonymous with the best arguments for American freedom from British tyranny.

There were other men, equally famous in their day, whose names became synonymous with proclaiming freedom from sin for those who would turn to Christ in faith. Jonathan Edwards. Gilbert Tennent. Theodore Frelinghuysen. Samuel Davies. George Whitefield. Whitefield became one of God's chosen instruments in popularizing the doctrine of the new birth in pre-Revolution America. He was also an early prophet of American independence.

In the subsequent trips Whitefield made to the North American colonies, his love and dedication to the material success and spiritual well-being of their inhabitants grew. He admired the foundation of religious freedom that had been laid, and he made full use of it on his preaching tours. From Savannah, Georgia, to New England, few towns were left untouched by the fire and force of Whitefield's proclamation of free grace.

Whitefield's visits to North America coincided with a series of spiritual awakenings that impacted the towns and cities of New England and the mid-Atlantic colonies beginning as early as the mid-1730s. Such times of revival were not uncommon in colonial history. In his sixty-year tenure as pastor of First Church, Northampton, Massachusetts (1669–1729), Solomon Stoddard experienced five "harvests" of souls in the surrounding community. Stoddard's grandson, Jonathan Edwards, took over for his grandfather in 1729. Under his leadership the church continued to experience periods of revival, which appear to be part of a more general movement of God in the colonies. Edwards did not lead alone.

Theodore Frelinghuysen came to America from Germany in 1719. Settling in the Raritan River valley of New Jersey, he became pastor of several Dutch Reformed churches and began preaching on the necessity of the new birth to his congregations. His boldness had two responses: resentment and bitter opposition by some, sincere repentance and conversion in the lives of others. Revival broke out in his congregations as early as 1726, with numerous young people responding first. This initial wave of converts was followed by deacons and elders responding in turn. His churches grew strong as many members came to the realization that they were unconverted and found salvation through Christ.

Across the Delaware River in Pennsylvania, Presbyterian William Tennent accepted the call to pastor several small churches in Bucks County. Within a few years, he built a log structure on his farm, in which he established a training academy for like-minded pastors. Detractors mockingly called it "the Log College" as it did not have the prestige or sophistication of institutions like Harvard or Yale. In spite of the derogatory comments, William successfully "homeschooled" his sons Gilbert, John, and William Jr. in biblical doctrine and trained a fresh generation of faithful Presbyterian evangelists and pastors for the North American colonies.

Gilbert Tennent moved to New Jersey, where he became pastor of a congregation in New Brunswick, not far from Frelinghuysen's churches. The two discovered that while hailing from two different denominations, they were brothers-in-arms in proclaiming the gospel. Tennent came to believe that many Presbyterian pastors were unconverted and therefore incapable of adequately preaching repentance and conversion to their congregations. In his famous sermon on "The Dangers of an Unconverted Ministry," Tennent urges prayer for unconverted pastors and their congregations and gives permission for people attending their churches to leave and seek churches shepherded by faithful pastors. Like his father and Frelinghuysen, Gilbert's principle emphasis in preaching was the need for personal repentance and conversion.

Samuel Davies was a graduate of Samuel Blair's training academy in Chester County, Pennsylvania. Blair, a pastor in the area, allowed Whitefield to preach in his churchyard. Inspired by the Grand Itinerant, Blair began a "log college" based on that of William Tennent. One of Blair's prized students, Davies took the message of new life through Christ to the American South. Moving to Virginia in 1748, Davies successfully petitioned for the freedom of Dissenting pastors to proclaim the gospel in the Commonwealth dominated by the Church of England. More irenic than his northern colleagues, Davies rarely exchanged ill words with his opponents as he logically appealed to both the head and heart of his hearers.

Arguably the greatest native-born factor in what would come to be known as the Great Awakening was Stoddard's grandson and successor, Jonathan Edwards. Edwards served as his grandfather's assistant for two years prior to taking over upon Stoddard's death in 1729. While most famous in American culture for his sermon "Sinners in the Hands of an Angry God," it was his sermon on "Justification by Faith" that God used to spur a revival that broke out in Northampton in 1734 and 1735. Edwards wrote an important account of the awakening in his "A Faithful Narrative of the Surprising Work of God," in which he describes several cases of conversion, noting the similarities and collating his conclusions. In it, Edwards writes much as a journalist, recording the facts as he saw them. Later, as the revivals spread and began to draw the attention of supporters and detractors, Edwards would move from being merely a reporter to being an apologist in defense of the revivals. His "Distinguishing Marks of a Work of the Spirit of God" is a classic argument for assessing when God is at work in a revival of true religion like the Great Awakening. Edwards did not convince all detractors, but his preaching, documentation, and leadership of the revivals put him at the forefront of this "surprising work of God." Whitefield's partnership with these colonial revival leaders coupled with his love for and commitment to the American people provide mounting evidence that, while he was a native of England, America was quickly becoming his adopted homeland.

Students of American history have learned that the Founding Fathers knew of each other's work and labored together in the cause of freedom. Students should be equally aware that the leaders of the Great Awakening knew of each other's work, corresponded with each other, and in many cases knew one another personally. On his previous trip to America, Whitefield had met Frelinghuysen and several members of the Tennent family and was impressed by the men of God he met on both sides of the Delaware River. On this trip, the Grand Itinerant met America's foremost theologian, Jonathan Edwards. Edwards opened not only his pulpit to Whitefield, but also his home. Whitefield called Edwards "a solid, excellent Christian" and "felt great satisfaction" at being entertained in the Edwards's home.

As in England, Whitefield found ready audiences in the churches of Dissenting pastors and in the fields and town squares of North America. A sense of that excitement is captured in the words of Nathan Cole, a farmer from Middletown, Connecticut, who recorded his thoughts concerning the day George Whitefield came to town:

In the morning about 8 or 9 of the Clock there came a messenger and said Mr. Whitefield preached at Hartford and Weathersfield yesterday and is to preach at Middletown this morning at ten of the Clock, I was in my field at Work, I dropt my tool that I had in my hand and ran home to my wife telling her to make ready quickly to go and hear Mr. Whitefield preach at Middletown, then ran to my pasture for my horse with all my might; fearing that I should be too late; having my horse I with my wife soon mounted the horse and went forward as fast as I thought the horse could bear, and when my horse got much out of breath I would get down and put my wife on the Saddle and bid her ride as fast as she could and not Stop or Slack for me except I bade her and so I would run until I was much out of breath; and then mount my horse again, and so I did several times to favour my horse; we improved every moment to get along as if we were fleeing for our lives; all the while fearing we should be too late to hear the Sermon, for we had twelve miles to ride double in little more than an hour. . . . And when we came within about half a mile of the road that comes down from Hartford, Weathersfield, and Stepney to Middletown; on high land I saw before me a Cloud or fog rising. I first thought it came from the great river, but as I came nearer the Road, I heard a noise something like a low rumbling thunder and presently found it was the noise of horses feet coming along the road and this Cloud was a Cloud of dust made by the Horses feet . . . every horse seemed to go with all his might to carry his rider to hear news from heaven for the saving of Souls. It made me tremble to see the Sight, how the world was in a Struggle. . . . When we got to the old meeting house there was a great multitude; it was said to be 3 or 4,000 of people assembled together. . . . When I saw Mr. Whitefield come upon the Scaffold he looked almost angelical, a young, slim, slender youth before some thousands of people with a bold undaunted countenance, and my hearing how God was with him everywhere as he came along it solemnized my mind, and put me into a trembling fear before he began to preach; for he looked as if he had been Cloathed with authority from the Great God, and a sweet solemn solemnity sat upon his brow. And my hearing him preach gave me a heart wound; by God's blessing my old foundation was broken up, and I saw that my righteousness would not save me; then I was convinced of the doctrine of Election and went right to quarrelling with God about it, because all that I could do would not save me; and he had decreed from Eternity who should be saved and who not.

Nathan Cole stands as one of the many who would point to a Whitefield sermon as the means God used to bring him to salvation. Crowds swelled wherever Whitefield preached. Four thousand in Middletown. Twenty thousand in Boston. Perhaps even more in Philadelphia. Skeptics might read the accounts of crowd size offered by Whitefield or even Nathan Cole and doubt their accuracy. Benjamin Franklin was such a skeptic until he conducted a field experiment during one of Whitefield's sermons preached from Philadelphia's courthouse steps. He listened at the outskirts of the crowd, then retreated beyond the crowd as far as he could still hear the sermon. By his subsequent calculation, Franklin determined Whitefield's voice could easily be heard by a crowd of at least thirty thousand people, which "reconciled" him "to the newspaper accounts of his having preached to twenty-five thousand people in the fields."

In his journal, Whitefield records the results of the revivals in glowing terms: "Numbers, great numbers, melted into tears." "The hearers were melted down." "Others were dissolved in tears." "Many were greatly affected." Many American souls were being radically changed by the power of the gospel. A change was coming over Whitefield's heart as well. He still called England "my native country" but admitted, "All things concur to convince me that America is to be my chief scene of action." George Whitefield had fallen in love with America as much as many Americans had fallen in love with him.

The effects of Whitefield's American preaching tours were tangible. Franklin wrote in the *Pennsylvania Gazette*,

The alteration in the face of religion here is altogether surprising. Never did the people show so great a willingness to attend sermons, nor the preachers greater zeal and diligence in performing the duties of their function. Religion is become the subject of most conventions. No books are in request but those of piety and devotion; and instead of idle songs and ballads, the people are everywhere entertaining themselves with psalms, hymns, and spiritual songs. All which, under God, is owing to the successful labours of the Reverend Mr. Whitefield.

Franklin continued his assessment of the positive change in America in his *Autobiography*:

> The multitudes of all sects and denominations that attended his sermons were enormous, and it was matter of speculation to me, who was one of the number, to observe the extraordinary influence of his oratory on his hearers, and how much they admir'd and respected him notwithstanding his common abuse of them, by assuring them they were naturally *half beasts and half devils*. It was wonderful to see the change soon made in the manners of our inhabitants. From being thoughtless or indifferent about religion, it seemed as if all the world were growing religious, so that one could not walk through the town in an evening without hearing psalms sung in different families at every street.

The glowing reports of revivals sweeping through the colonies should not be misinterpreted to indicate that this British colonial outpost had "become" Christian or even "religious." Franklin admitted that it "seemed" to be so, but recent scholarship has shown that while church membership grew, new churches were planted, and many people's lives were changed as a result of the Great Awakening, the fervor waned as the eighteenth century marched along. In fact, by the early nineteenth century, America would be ripe for a Second Great Awakening. As the second half of the eighteenth century dawned, many Americans who had recently focused on the freedom that comes through Christ turned their attention toward a new quest for freedom equally life changing and with a fervor no less religious.

The study of colonial America reveals the rich patchwork of religious diversity that characterized the American "quilt."

Colonies like Massachusetts were established by individuals seeking the freedom to worship God as their consciences dictated. Others were founded as havens for Dissenters of various stripes: Maryland for Roman Catholics, Rhode Island for Baptists. Still others, like Pennsylvania, opened their doors to people regardless of the creed they adopted. During the course of the 1700s, several things became abundantly clear on the American religious scene. First, America provided a wide variety of church options for those seeking a place to worship. Back home in England, the Church of England was the established church. In Whitefield's time, one could affiliate with a Dissenting congregation, but such groups were relatively few and far between and had to be licensed by the government. America provided not only the traditional English assortment of churches—Anglican, Presbyterian, Quaker, Congregationalist—but other European options as well: Lutheran, Dutch Reformed, Roman Catholic.

A second characteristic of Christianity in eighteenth-century America was that, while Whitefield could rejoice that the "work of God" in the colonies was "carried on here" by those who preached the "doctrines of election and final perseverance of the saints," he and other preachers offered God's grace "freely" and "to all." While on the surface some may see this as an inconsistency, it is perfectly in line with Whitefield's Reformed theology. Preaching was the means ordained by God to reach the vast majority of the elect. Since Whitefield was not privy to divine "inside information" as to who the elect in any given crowd might be, he offered free grace to all, understanding all the while that only the elect could respond. It is conceivable that many of his hearers would not catch the theological intricacies of his doctrine, especially when they heard his emotional appeals. "Get acquaintance with God, then, and be at peace," thundered Whitefield, "My business . . . is to tell you that Christ is willing to be reconciled to you. Will any of you be reconciled to Jesus Christ?" In the same sermon, Whitefield also said, "May God influence your hearts to come to him," but two sentences later says, "God may make use of me as a means of persuading some of you to come to the Lord Jesus Christ." He concludes another of his published sermons with the appeal, "Why, why will you die? Why will you not come unto him, that you may have life?" By emphasizing the role of personal choice in salvation, Whitefield's preaching signals a shift from the precise Calvinistic theology of Jonathan Edwards toward a popular Americanized version palatable to freedom-loving patriots.

Liberty, in all its forms, was a third characteristic of American religious and popular culture. The North American colonies were a long way from England. Governors of the Crown oversaw the colonies, but the king never set foot in the colonies. Those same governors gave leadership to the Anglican churches in the colonies, but there was no resident bishop in North America prior to the Revolution. Family and village ties were stretched thin over the wide Atlantic. Couple the loosening of these ties with the uncompromising tone of Parliament toward American patriots, especially relating to issues of taxation and representation, and the result was fertile soil for the planting and growth of the Revolutionary movement.

As his roots grew deeper into the American culture, Whitefield became a prophetic voice regarding the colonies' place in the world. In one of his lesser-known sermons penned a full generation before the Revolution, Whitefield sings the praises of "liberty" in the context of a recently failed French invasion of England. Seeing Roman Catholicism much as American patriots would later view the English Crown, Whitefield warns his listeners what "would have been" if British armies had not defeated those who would have taken away their liberties. Missionary monks would have "invaded" England and her colonies. Foreign bishops would have been placed in English dioceses. Parents would have been forced to have their children educated in Roman schools. The proclamation of the gospel would have ceased. Preachers would have been forced to proclaim "antichristian doctrines" like salvation by works and transubstantiation. And worst of all, "How soon should we have been deprived of that invaluable blessing, liberty of conscience, and been obliged to commence (what they falsely call) catholics, or submit to all the tortures which a bigoted zeal, guided by the most cruel principles, could possibly invent? Ironically, Whitefield preached this sermon in Philadelphia, the "cradle of liberty," in July 1746 only months after the Catholic armies had been defeated in Scotland. In 1746 Whitefield painted French Roman Catholics as enemies of freedom and liberty in all its forms. Thirty years later, American patriots from Thomas Paine to Thomas Jefferson would use the same language to paint the English Crown and Parliament as equally dangerous enemies of liberty.

When British interests were threatened in North America, Whitefield proved a capable recruiter and *de facto* military chaplain. From their settlement Fort Louisburg on Nova Scotia, the French navy harassed New England and disrupted English shipping. Colonel William Pepperell was charged with raising a British invasion force to attack the French base in spring 1745, and the troops approached Whitefield to persuade men to enlist and to provide the expedition with a motto for their flag. He provided the motto, "Never despair. Christ leads." He encouraged "great numbers" to enlist. Louisburg fell to the British. With such a positive outcome, it is not surprising that other military officers looked to Whitefield for good luck. On his way to invade Canada in September 1775, General Benedict Arnold stopped at Old South Presbyterian Church in Newburyport, Massachusetts. Aaron Burr was also a part of the invasion force. George Whitefield, dead since 1770, was interred beneath the pulpit of the church. After worshiping with the congregation, Arnold asked the pastor if he could see the sainted remains. Who could refuse a general's request? When the crypt was opened and the coffin lid removed, Arnold's men removed Whitefield's collar and cuffs to take them into battle much like Israel's armies took the Ark of the Covenant or Crusaders took the relics of a saint. Arnold's troops were soundly defeated.

During the Seven Years' War (better known to Americans as the French and Indian Wars), Whitefield wrote a powerful and passionate letter to Lady Pepperell, whose husband was again leading British troops into harm's way. From England he wrote,

> You and my other New England friends had the prayers of thousands. How did I wish to be transported to America! How did I long to stir up all against the common enemy, and to be made instrumental of doing my dear country some little service! Dear New England,—dear Boston lies upon my heart! Surely the Lord will not give it over into the hands of the enemy. He has too many praying people there, for such a dreadful catastrophe.

One assumes that when Whitefield, writing from England to another British subject, wishes to do "my dear country some little service," he is speaking about his homeland. Yet with the mentioning of New England twice and "dear Boston" once, it would be understandable for contemporary readers to assume that the "dear country" for which he prayed was still twenty years away from her nativity! Of that nation yet to be born, Whitefield expressed his opinion, in a sermon preached from the pulpit of Bethesda, that the colonies of America were likely to become "one of the most opulent and powerful empires in the world." This expressed by a man who died five full years before America's fight for independence began.

While recognized as a champion of liberty by American colonists, Whitefield still saw himself primarily as a preacher of the good news wherever God might send him. He was not a political activist or theorist, though he was "adopted" by various sides of political debate. He may have felt much more at home in the American colonies, but he continued to see himself as a faithful subject of the British Crown. He capably led revivals in both his adopted homeland and the land of his birth. Whitefield had become an international celebrity.

Leadership of the revivals on both sides of the Atlantic put Whitefield in the spotlight for both supporters and detractors to see. Just as in America, the crowds flocked to hear him. Many responded to his pleas to come to Christ. Funds flowed in to support the Bethesda Orphan House. But as Whitefield drew crowds away from actors, musicians, and hucksters, those who preferred their kind of entertainment rather than Whitefield's sought to drown him out or to silence him completely. Hecklers interrupted his sermons. Drummers and trumpeters tried to drown out the one who could be heard by upwards of thirty thousand people. The more violent hecklers hurled bricks, rocks, sticks, even parts of dead animals. Whitefield would not be silenced. Even an assassination attempt would not dissuade him from proclaiming God's Word.

4.1 This unflattering portrait suggests Whitefield was a charlatan who simply sought to control his audiences. It does rightly portray the fact that Whitefield was cross-eyed.

Writers and actors took potshots at Whitefield in print and on stage. Playwright Samuel Foote lampooned White-field in his 1760 play, *The Minor.* Mother Cole, a madam modeled on a contemporary of Foote, has fallen under the spell of the evangelist Dr. Squintum. Foote employed the very name of this character as a thinly veiled reference to Whitefield, who was notably cross-eyed, most likely due to a childhood illness. Dr. Squintum never appears onstage, but the main character, Shift, parodies the itinerant who helped to save Mother Cole's soul but not enough to change her lifestyle.

Joseph Reed picked up where Foote left off in his *The Register's Office.* In the second act, another madam, Mrs. Snarewell, a new Methodist convert, explains that her rheumatism kept her up all night but that the Methodist minister attended to her needs. She gladly gives the minister, Mr. Watchlight, all her money so that he might improve his church. The parallels between Foote's play and Reed's were so obvious that Reed was forced to defend himself regularly against charges of plagiarism.

Even fellow Anglican priest Richard Graves tried his hand at satirizing the Methodists in general and George Whitefield in particular. In his 1773 novel *The Spiritual Quixote, or the Summer's Ramble of Mr. Geoffry Wildgoose,* Wildgoose "hears the call" and sets out on an itinerant preaching tour to save souls. He chooses the lifestyle largely because he cannot find anything more interesting to do.

Such high-profile lampooning, while angering some of Whitefield's supporters, was in a sense high praise from those targeting Whitefield. Quiet parish priests who minded their own business while caring for their flocks attracted little attention from satirists. A field-preaching itinerant evangelist, wildly popular in England and her colonies, provided an easy target. It was proof of Whitefield's effectiveness and popularity. Perhaps it indicated professional jealousy. Whitefield drew larger crowds than the London stage. He preached to larger audiences than Graves ever would in his local parishes. Famous actor David Garrick envied his black-robed competitor and mused that he would willingly pay five hundred pounds if he could say, "Oh!" like Whitefield. In an ironic twist, the man who turned his back on a stage career when he came to Christ preached God's good news to far larger crowds than he ever would have starring in one of Foote's or Reed's plays.

Leading revivals on an international scale brought many into the kingdom of God. It brought Whitefield to the attention of adoring fans and bitter rivals. Whitefield masterfully used both controversies and personal connections to spread the message of salvation through Christ. Sometimes the controversy and the connection were packaged together.

5

"CATHOLIC SPIRIT": CONTROVERSY AND CONNECTIONS SPREAD THE REVIVALS

On a trip to Oxford, England, several years ago, my family and I visited sites important to the lives of the friends and colleagues C. S. Lewis and J. R. R. Tolkien. We visited their homes, toured their respective colleges, and ate in the pubs they frequented. We worshiped in churches and cathedrals where they worshiped, even sitting in the very pew at Holy Trinity Church in Headington Quarry where Lewis sat with his brother each Sunday. We paid our respects at the cemeteries where their earthly bodies rest. We sensed that Oxford itself provided an environment uniquely suited to the growth of their friendship.

Over two hundred years prior to the friendships forged by members of the Inklings, George Whitefield, Charles Wesley, and John Wesley nurtured a similarly deep friendship beneath the "dreaming spires" of Oxford. The Wesley brothers were instrumental in Whitefield's early spiritual growth, and the three worked together through the "Holy Club" performing various works of mercy for prisoners, the poor, and the sick in and around Oxford. All three entered the priesthood of the Church of England and spent time in Georgia as missionaries, albeit relatively unsuccessfully in the case of the Wesleys. The three eventually became partners in proclaiming the gospel wherever the opportunity presented itself: in local churches, prisons, and fields, or at places of execution.

Looking at the similarities is not meant to suggest that Whitefield and the Wesleys were identical triplets. The trio had noticeable major differences. Charles Wesley was an accomplished poet and lyricist who, along with contemporaries Isaac Watts, Philip Doddridge, and Augustus Toplady, kept English Christians of all denominations singing throughout the eighteenth century and beyond. While John Wesley translated some hymns of German Pietists, he is best known for his organizational abilities. Whitefield, a gifted evangelist, left the organization of converts up to people like John Wesley, who artfully brought them together into bands, classes, and societies for Bible study, prayer, and mutual accountability. All three knew success as preachers, but Whitefield's preaching bears closer resemblance to the type of preaching still heard from pulpits in many of today's churches. John Wesley's sermons are tightly crafted logical treatises appealing more to the "head." Whitefield's narrative sermons, while far from illogical, were squarely aimed at the "heart." Whitefield's publishing interests were limited to his journals and sermons, while John Wesley wrote theological treatises, foreign language grammars, and even a book on homeopathic medicine. While writing no systematic theology in the traditional sense, Wesley did think and write systematically about theology. Whitefield had his own strongly held theological views, and it is at the intersection of their respective theologies that the friendship between Whitefield and the Wesleys deteriorated.

5.1 Whitefield had deep theological differences with John and Charles Wesley, yet his contributions to the founding of Methodism are recognized by his inclusion in the *Illustrated History of Methodism*.

The theological differences between Whitefield and Wesley can be stated simply enough: Whitefield came to interpret Scripture from a Calvinistic perspective while Wesley adopted an Arminian view. It is not surprising then that the two would disagree on such important doctrines as election, the extent of Christ's atonement, the perseverance of the saints, and sanctification. What may be more surprising is that they were able to keep the differences "under wraps" as long as they did and that the differences did not create a permanent rift in their friendship. They succeeded because of the doctrine upon which they did agree and because they realized they were part of building with God something even bigger than the things that could have easily turned them apart.

Whitefield cautiously addressed their differences as early as 1739. In July he wrote to Wesley, wondering, "How shall I tell the Dissenters I do not approve of their doctrines, without wronging my own soul? How shall I tell them I do, without contradicting my honoured friend, whom I desire to love as my own soul?" The very next month, Wesley resorted once again to casting a lot to determine God's will, and he decided to "preach and print" his controversial sermon, "Free Grace." In it, he attacked every doctrine of grace Whitefield held dear: election, the limited atonement, and the perseverance of the saints. Up until this time, the two had endeavored to keep their differences private. In Whitefield's view, Wesley had changed the game. He prepared and sent his response to Wesley.

Written from the safe confines of Bethesda in Savannah on Christmas Eve 1740, Whitefield addresses a letter to Wesley refuting his sermon point by point. He first takes Wesley to task for "tempting God" by leaving such an important decision up to casting a lot. On one occasion in 1739, Whitefield participated with fellow Methodists in casting a lot, but it was far from normal practice for him. He chides Wesley by saying, "A due exercise of religious prudence, without a lot, would have directed you in that matter."

Next, he challenges Wesley on his choice of Scripture text. Whitefield is surprised he has chosen to preach against election using Romans 8, a classic text normally used to argue for election as a scriptural doctrine. "Honoured Sir, how could it enter into your heart to choose a text to disprove the doctrine of election out of the 8th of Romans, where this doctrine is so plainly asserted?" Whitefield continues firing:

I frankly acknowledge, I believe the doctrine of reprobation, in this view, that God intends to give saving grace, through Jesus Christ, only to a certain number, and that the rest of mankind, after the fall of Adam, being justly left of God to continue in sin, will at last suffer that eternal death, which is its proper wages.

This is the established doctrine of Scripture, and acknowledged as such in the 17th article of the Church of England, as Bishop Burnet himself confesses; yet dear Mr. Wesley absolutely denies.

Whitefield continues the defense of his views against Wesley's accusation that if the doctrine of election is true, then "all preaching [is in] vain." Far from it, argues Whitefield: "How is preaching needless to them that are elected, when the gospel is designed by God himself to be the power of God unto their eternal salvation? And since we know not who are elect and who reprobate, we are to preach promiscuously to all." God said, "Preach the gospel." Whitefield answered, "Yes, I will!"

Wesley had argued that the doctrine of election "tends to destroy that holiness which is the end of all the ordinances of God." Turning the tables on one who held holiness in such high regard, Whitefield counters,

I thought that one who carries perfection to such an exalted pitch as dear Mr. Wesley does would know, that a true lover of the Lord Jesus Christ would strive to be holy for the sake of being holy, and work for Christ out of love and gratitude, without any regard to the rewards of heaven, or fear of hell. . . . Do not the elect know that the more good works they do, the greater will be their reward? And is not that encouragement enough to set them upon, and cause them to persevere in working for Jesus Christ?

Countering Wesley's point that election "tends to destroy the comforts of religion" and "the happiness of Christianity,"

Whitefield quotes the seventeenth Article of Religion of the Church of England: "The godly consideration of predestination, and election in Christ, is full of sweet, pleasant, unspeakable comfort to godly persons, and such as feel in themselves the working of the Spirit of Christ." When Wesley charges Whitefield with the "uncomfortable thought" of "thousands and millions of men, without any preceding offence or fault of theirs, were unchangeably doomed to everlasting burnings," Whitefield reminds him that no one is innocent: Adam's sin makes everyone guilty. Wesley accuses supporters of the doctrine of election with endangering Christianity, as through God's "unchangeable decree, one part of mankind must be saved, though the Christian revelation were not in being." Whitefield responds, "How does that follow? Since it is only by the Christian revelation that we are acquainted with God's design of saving his church by the death of his Son." "Dear sir," Whitefield concludes, "for Jesus Christ's sake, consider how you dishonour God by denying election. You plainly make salvation depend not on *God's free grace*, but on *man's free will*; and if thus, it is more than probable, Jesus Christ would not have had the satisfaction of seeing the fruit of his death in the eternal salvation of one soul. Our preaching would then be in vain, and all invitations for people to believe in him would also be in vain." Whitefield held out hope that in heaven, "I shall see dear Mr. Wesley convinced of election and everlasting love. And it often fills me with pleasure to think how I shall behold you casting your crown down at the feet of the Lamb, and as it were filled with a holy blushing for opposing the divine sovereignty in the manner you have done."

For much of the next year, there is no existing correspondence between Whitefield and Wesley—a fact that surely pained both men, who had worked so closely together. Wesley, at least, feared that their friendship had been irreparably damaged: "[Whitefield] told me, he and I preached two different gospels, and therefore he not only would not join with or give me the right hand of fellowship, but was resolved publicly to preach against me and my brother, wheresoever he preached at all." And only days later, Wesley expressed that Whitefield "had said enough of what was wholly foreign to the question, to make an open (and probably irreparable) breach between him and me." Fortunately for their friendship and the cause of the spread of the gospel, Wesley proved to be no prophet!

It was Whitefield who made the first overtures toward reconciliation. He writes passionately from Scotland on October 10, 1741,

> I have for a long time expected that you would have sent me an answer to my last; but I suppose that you are afraid to correspond with me, because I revealed your secret about the lot. Though much may be said for my doing it, yet I am sorry now, that any such thing dropped from my pen, and I humbly ask pardon. I find I love you as much as ever, and pray God, if it be his blessed will, that we may be all united together. It hath been for some days upon my heart to write to you, and this morning I receive a letter from brother H[owell Harris], telling me how he had conversed with you and your dear brother. May God remove all obstacles that now prevent our union! Though I hold particular election, yet I offer Jesus freely to every individual soul. You may carry sanctification to what degrees you will, only I cannot agree that the in-being of sin is to be destroyed in this life. . . . May all disputings cease, and each of us talk of nothing but Jesus, and him crucified! This is my resolution. The Lord be with your spirit. My love to brother C[harles], and all that love the glorious Emmanuel. I am, without dissimulation, ever yours, G.W.

Wesley was convinced of Whitefield's sincerity, believing that he possessed an "earnest desire of joining hand in hand with all that love the Lord Jesus Christ." Their actions spoke louder than words. Over the course of three days in January 1750, the two traded preaching and worship-leading responsibilities at West Street Chapel. "One more stumbling block is removed," wrote Wesley. Over the next few years, Whitefield occasionally visited Wesley, and they agreed to "join hand in hand to promote the cause of our common Master." They had successfully "agreed to disagree" and to work together on the common goal of proclaiming the good news of salvation through Jesus Christ. Charles Wesley put the healing of their friendship in more poetic terms.

> Come on, my Whitefield! (since the strife is past,
> And friends at first are friends again at last)
> Our hands, our hearts, and counsels let us join
> In mutual league, t'advance the work divine,
> Our one contention now, our single aim,
> To pluck poor souls as brands out of the flame;
> To spread the victory of that bloody cross,
> And gasp our latest breath in the Redeemer's cause.

Whitefield continued to nurture his relationship with Wesley even though they had significant theological differences. But this was a pattern that marked Whitefield's ministry. He sought to cultivate positive, cooperative relationships with people from across the theological spectrum. He did so by retaining his theological integrity and by confronting unbiblical teaching, while at the same time seeking to build as broad a base of evangelical agreement as possible. Those who were willing to join with Whitefield in spreading the good news were welcome to participate in the revivals. Whitefield also welcomed members of the contemporary media, whatever they believed, as long as they partnered with him in spreading the news of the revival's growth.

Benjamin Franklin, scientist, philosopher, and statesman, was part of the contemporary media that aided Whitefield in the spread of news regarding the revivals in the colonies. As publisher of the well-read *Pennsylvania Gazette*, Franklin quickly learned what sold papers; and George Whitefield sold not only papers, but sermons and journals as well. Whitefield and Franklin nurtured a mutually beneficial relationship. Franklin was in the business of printing and selling reading material. Whitefield provided plenty of material that the reading public eagerly devoured. Whitefield helped Franklin to make a profit. Franklin helped Whitefield the prophet develop new audiences.

As discussion continues to rage over the Christian faith (or lack thereof) of the Founding Fathers, Benjamin Franklin's forthcoming honesty is refreshing. He left no room for doubt regarding where he stood in relationship to the Christian faith. During his teenage years, Franklin read works written against Deism that had an unintended consequence. Rather than convincing him of the truths of revealed religion, they convinced him of the "truth" of Deism. As an adult, Franklin occasionally attended worship, once for "five weeks in a row," and believed the practice of worship to be a proper and useful thing "when rightly conducted." Later in life, as a fully convinced Deist, Franklin put together the outline of a creed that he believed were the points of agreement upon which all the world's religions could agree: "That there is one God, who made all things. That he governs the world by his providence. That he ought to be worshiped by adoration, prayer, and thanksgiving. But that the most acceptable service of God is doing good to man. That the soul is immortal. And that God will certainly reward virtue and punish vice, either here or hereafter."

Whitefield would have had little problem with Franklin's theology . . . as far as it went! But being the dedicated evangelist that he was, Whitefield was committed to sharing the good news of salvation through Christ with everyone, including Benjamin Franklin, in the hope that even he might be part of God's elect. Franklin counted Whitefield a friend and "a perfectly honest man," but writes of the unsuccessful attempts at his conversion: "He us'd, indeed, sometimes to pray for my conversion, but never had the satisfaction of believing that his prayers were heard. Ours was a mere civil friendship, sincere on both sides, and lasted to his death." Franklin actually invited Whitefield to lodge with him on one of his trips through Philadelphia. Seizing the witnessing opportunity, Whitefield told Franklin that if he "made that kind offer for Christ's sake, he should not miss of a reward." Franklin, not to be outdone, retorted, "Don't let me be mistaken; it was not for Christ's sake, but for your sake." He would later write to Whitefield,

> Your frequently repeated wishes for my eternal, as well as my temporal happiness, are very obliging, and I can only thank you for them and offer you mine in return. I have myself no doubt, that I shall enjoy as much of both as is proper for me. That Being, who gave me existence, and through almost threescore years has been continually showering his favors upon me, whose very chastisements have been blessings to me; can I doubt that he loves me? And, if he loves me, can I doubt that he will go on to take care of me, not only here but hereafter? This to some may seem presumption; to me it appears the best grounded hope; hope of the future built on experience of the past.

While Whitefield would disagree with both the premises and conclusions of Franklin's theology, he helped to expand Franklin's business, while Franklin helped the spread of Whitefield's message. All told, Franklin published eight installments of Whitefield's journals, nine editions of his sermons, and ultimately his memoirs, not to mention countless newspaper articles and advertisements. He financially supported Whitefield's orphan house and was instrumental in the building of a lecture hall he made available to Whitefield and to "any preacher of any religious persuasion who might desire to say something to the people at Philadelphia." Franklin's lecture hall would eventually become the foundation of the University of Pennsylvania, and a statue of Whitefield still graces the campus of the Ivy League institution.

5.2 Statue on the campus of the University of Pennsylvania. The roots of this Ivy League institution rest in a building funded by Benjamin Franklin for use by Whitefield and any other preacher of any faith.

It would surprise few if they discovered that Whitefield carried on cordial relationships with those with whom he had the most in common. Friendships with John Wesley and Benjamin Franklin may surprise some, but many might suspect Whitefield to have deeper friendships with those from the same theological camp. Whitefield did develop lasting friendships with many American pastors from the Reformed tradition. But it is interesting to note that not all Calvinists counted Whitefield as a friend and valued coworker.

Howell Harris did, and the feeling was mutual. Harris was one of the key leaders in the evangelical revivals in Wales during Whitefield's lifetime. He had been preaching in the fields of Wales for a number of years before introducing the practice to Whitefield and encouraging him to try it. Their friendship began as early as 1738 and would last through their lifetimes. Whitefield not only found theological kinship in his relationship with Harris, but also found that Harris had a "catholic spirit": a willingness to work together with like-minded fellow believers in kingdom work even when they may have held some different theological opinions. In fact, when Whitefield and Wesley parted company over their theological debate, it was Howell Harris who worked diligently to bring them back together, as his heart broke over the thought of the work of God in the British revivals coming to an end over their disagreement.

Whitefield may have shared theological agreement with members of the Reformed family, but that did not mean that he could always work together with them as effectively as with Howell Harris or even John Wesley! On one of his preaching tours through Scotland, Whitefield was introduced to Ralph and Ebenezer Erskine—brothers who had been ordained by the Scottish Kirk but had subsequently withdrawn to form a separatist Associate Presbytery. Strongly Calvinistic, the Erskines believed there should be no "tyranny" imposed by presbytery or synod, and that each local congregation should be free to choose its own pastor. While in complete theological agreement with the Erskines, Whitefield's commitment to his own Church of England would not allow him to end that relationship in order to unite officially with the Erskines' Associate Presbytery. Whitefield honored them for their sound theology: "I bless God, his spirit has convinced me of our eternal election through the Son, of our free justification through faith in his blood, of our sanctification as the consequence of that, and of our final perseverance and glorification as the result of all. These I am persuaded God had joined together: these, neither men nor devils shall ever be able to put asunder." Yet, while complimenting them on their sound doctrine, Whitefield would not leave the Church of England just to please the Erskines.

> I come only as an occasional preacher, to preach the simple gospel to all that are willing to hear me, of whatever denomination. It will be wrong in me to join in a reformation as to church government, any further than I have light given me from above. If I am quite neuter as to that in my preaching, I cannot see how it can hinder or retard any design you may have on foot. My business seems to be, to evangelize, to be a Presbyter at large.

The Eskines were not pleased with Whitefield's decision, and they let him know he was not welcome any longer in their pulpits. Whitefield wrote to Ebenezer expressing his understanding and his concern.

> It is some concern to me, that our difference as to outward things, should cut off our sweet fellowship and communion with each other. God knows my heart, I highly value and honour you. . . . I do assure you I love you and your brethren more than ever. I applaud your zeal for God; and though, in some respects, I think it not according to knowledge, and

to be leveled frequently against me, yet indeed I feel no resentment in my heart, and should joyfully sit down and hear you and your brethren preach. I salute them all; and pray our common Lord to give us all a right judgment in all things. . . . O when shall the time come, when the watchmen will see eye to eye?

Whitefield believed his commission to include preaching the gospel of God's free grace wherever an audience might be found. He was sure that God did not want issues such as church government to stand in the way.

Having been raised in the humble surroundings of the Bell Inn in Gloucester, Whitefield had no difficulty preaching to the regulars in a public house. He was comfortable sharing the good news with rough-and-tumble miners near Bristol, with card-playing, foul-mouthed sailors on the high seas, or with backwoods colonists on the North American frontier. He carried on cordial relationships with people from many theological camps: Anglicans, Dissenters, even Deists. Whitefield's popularity helped to make him either a hero or a target of various members of these groups. But it also opened doors to another group of people that Wesley and others in the Methodist movement had difficulty accessing.

According to *The Gentlemen's Library* published in 1760, "True honor, though it be a different principle from religion, is that which produces the same effects." Much of polite society in eighteenth-century England affirmed that "the spirit of a gentleman, and the spirit of religion" were not only compatible, but the extent of true Christianity. Focusing as extensively as they did on ministry to the poor, prisoners, and the sick, Wesley's Methodists did not attract much attention from the upper crust of British society. Gentlemen and gentlewomen, largely members of the High Church party of the Church of England, might send a few pounds to the relief of the downtrodden but were unlikely to attend a Methodist class meeting or to be impressed by preachers who called them to a life of austerity. But a popular preacher who was in all the papers and who had an international reputation—that might be a different story!

Key to Whitefield's introduction into the upper echelons of British society was Selina Hastings, Countess of Huntingdon. A member of the nobility in her own right, she married the Earl of Huntingdon and fulfilled the responsibilities that were expected of a woman of her station. Coming to faith in Christ through the witness of her sister-in-law, Lady Huntingdon became a member of the Fetter Lane Society and a key ally and supporter of the Methodist movement. Her husband died in 1746, and she remained a widow the rest of her life. She dedicated the remainder of her life to the spread of the gospel through the ministry of George Whitefield.

Appointed her chaplain in 1748, Whitefield accepted his new appointment with relish. Not only would it bring him into contact with people of means who could support the orphan house in Savannah, it opened doors to preach the life-changing gospel to an entirely new audience. His hearers at the Countess's estate reads like a "who's who" of English nobility: the Dutchess of Marlborough, Lord Chesterfield, Lord Bolingbroke, Lady Suffolk, Lord Chatham, Horace Walpole. Writing to the Countess of Bath, Whitefield rejoiced, "It would please you to see the assemblies at her ladyship's house. They are brilliant ones indeed. The prospect of catching some of the rich, in the gospel net, is very promising." Whitefield definitely had big fish to catch! While there are no records of his "landing" any noblemen for the cause of Christ, he certainly regaled them with his stirring sermons and stories of how God was moving in the North American colonies, saving sinners and reclaiming precious orphans. He was much more successful leading several notable noblewomen to Christ, some of whom opened their homes as preaching places.

Lady Huntingdon's support for Whitefield and the revivals went far deeper than merely opening her home to him and introducing him to her wealthy friends. The Countess personally funded the founding of dozens of chapels throughout England dedicated to the preaching of the gospel, going so far as to appoint the preachers herself. In 1768 she established a college at Trevecca, Wales, dedicated to the training of like-minded pastors. George Whitefield preached the dedication sermon. Her patronage extended to Whitefield's London Tabernacle on Tottenham Court Road in London and the Bethesda Orphan House in Savannah, and it helped to relieve the perennial financial burden felt by the Grand Itinerant. Luke Tyerman, an early biographer of both John Wesley and Whitefield, suggests that no one could possibly "estimate the service rendered to the church by the despised Whitefield and his female prelate, the grand, stately, strong-minded, godly, and self-sacrificing Countess of Huntingdon."

Today's churches are consistently reminded of the importance of "relational evangelism": building networks and friendships that one day might well be used as a platform from which to share the gospel. Whitefield's example of building such relationships, while over two hundred years old, serves as a model for contemporary churches. Whitefield successfully nurtured relationships with like-minded Christians and formed a broad-based revival network that minimized denominational connections. That is not to say that Whitefield was unconcerned about theology! His theology was rooted in the Scriptures and shaped by the rich Reformed tradition. While "agreeing to disagree" over some deeply held theological convictions, Whitefield cultivated relationships that served to reach vast numbers of hearers and readers with the good news.

Whitefield recognized and harnessed the power of the press in an age when publishing was just coming into its own in colonial America. His friendship with one of America's earliest "media moguls" assured that he would provide Benjamin Franklin with a steady stream of publishable material while Franklin provided the distribution mechanism for Whitefield's message. Whitefield was on the cutting edge in the use of the "social media" of his day.

Benjamin Franklin was not the only high-profile friend of George Whitefield. Courting America's foremost printer and leading thinker had its benefits. But so did the friendship of Lady Huntingdon. Through friendship with her, Whitefield was introduced to an entirely new audience that was largely unreached by other evangelicals of the day. Whitefield's international popularity opened the door, and he enthusiastically walked through it. But there is no hint that Whitefield ever watered down the message to suit his aristocratic audience. They, too, needed to hear that they were sinners, ruined by Adam's fall, redeemed only by the free grace of God through Jesus Christ.

Whitefield's willingness to nurture relationships with individuals across the theological spectrum suggests that he was part of something much larger than he ever suspected. As Mark Noll has pointed out, Whitefield's spiritual heritage included Calvinism (especially of the English Puritan variety), European Pietism, and High Church Anglicanism— three influences that directly fed the British evangelical revivals and the Great Awakening in North America. In his *The Rise of Evangelicalism: The Age of Edwards, Whitefield and the Wesleys,* Noll suggests the key points at which Whitefield may be considered one of the "fathers" of the evangelical movement. He contributed a strong evangelical emphasis to the major denominations represented in North America. He built bridges between evangelically minded members of less-than-evangelical denominations and those with traditional evangelical views. He served as an inspiration to future Baptist and Methodist leaders, all the while exhibiting an "extraordinary disregard" for church tradition. As with many contemporary evangelicals, he proved to possess an amazing entrepreneurial spirit coupled with a keen ability to innovate, which sometimes led to the proposing of more plans than he was able to implement. He understood the power of the contemporary media. His deep commitment to the spread of the gospel, while commendable, could be stained by a judgmental streak and an unwillingness to consider all the implications of Christian social ethics.[1] If not the father of contemporary evangelicalism, Whitefield was unquestionably one of its earliest shapers.

Whitefield continued to boldly proclaim the message to audiences, made up of nobility and commoner alike, on both sides of the Atlantic. For Whitefield, his message never grew old or wore thin, even though the messenger was beginning to wear out.

---

1. See Mark A. Noll, *A History of Christianity in the United States and Canada* (Grand Rapids: Eerdmans, 1992), 108–9.

6

"I WOULD RATHER WEAR OUT THAN RUST OUT": THE FINAL AMERICAN TOUR

George Whitefield was wearing out. It was a process that started early in his ministry and snowballed as he entered his fifth decade. Throughout his journals he recorded accounts of occasional sickness that, while they did not keep him down for long, were signs of the toll his unrelenting travel and preaching schedule were taking on his body. Even as a young man of twenty-four he wrote, "I had a thorn in the flesh sent to buffet me, being weak in body and deserted in mind. With great reluctance I rose and preached to about two thousand, at eight o'clock in the morning; then I retired to my bed again, with an unspeakable pressure upon my heart till noon." He would often write of the "inward visitations and bodily indisposition" that he faced, normally after several marathon days of preaching, traveling, and offering spiritual counsel into the early hours of the morning. His preferred remedy was working up a good "pulpit sweat."

Whitefield planned a final trip to America. It would be his seventh voyage to North America. He preached his last sermon on English soil from the Tottenham Court Road Tabernacle on the very spot where, a year earlier, he had stood to preach at his wife's funeral. He admitted to his London flock that this trip would be his thirteenth across the Atlantic, and that it would be "a little difficult at this time of life." He was fully aware of the ravages that time and exertion were taking on his body.

> Some of you, I doubt not, will be gone to him before my return; but, my dear brethren, my dear hearers, never mind that; we shall part, but it will be to meet again for ever. I dare not meet you now, I cannot bear your coming to me, to part from me; it cuts me to the heart, and quite overcomes me, but by and by all parting will be over, and all tears shall be wiped away from our eyes. God grant that none that weep now at my parting, may weep at our meeting at the day of judgment. . . . If you never heard his voice before, God grant you may hear it now; that I may have this comfort when I am gone, that I had the last time of my leaving you, that some souls are awakened at the parting sermon. O that it may be a farewell sermon to you; that it may be a means of your taking a farewell of the world, the lust of the flesh, the lust of the eyes and the pride of life.

He arrived at his beloved Bethesda in January 1770 and spent much of the year in its comfortable surroundings. Bethesda was finally "debt-free," and Whitefield hoped to establish a college at the same location. He went so far as to prepare the list of rules that would be followed in the daily operation of the school: morning and evening prayer every day, daily preaching of the Word, behavior expected of students, even the course of study. Sadly, Whitefield never saw his dream become a reality, and the dream died with him.

Whitefield loved Bethesda, but he loved preaching the gospel even more. During the early morning hours of April 24, Whitefield left Bethesda for the last time because "all must give way to Gospel ranging: Divine employ!" Throughout the late spring, summer, and early fall, Whitefield traveled north, preaching as he went in some of his favorite American locales, including Philadelphia and Boston. By the time he reached coastal Massachusetts in late September, it was obvious to many that he was entering the final days of his earthly pilgrimage. There would be no continuation of his "Gospel ranging" into Canada as he planned. There would be no return trip to Savannah.

6.1 A son of the Church of England, Whitefield gladly preached in established churches—until the doors were closed to him. Then he took his message outdoors.

On September 29, Whitefield preached in the town of Exeter, Massachusetts, in his favorite setting: outdoors. Written accounts indicate that someone in the crowd noticed his weakened condition and told him, "You are more fit to go to bed than to preach." Whitefield agreed, then, turning his gaze skyward, prayed, "Lord Jesus, I am weary in thy work, but not of thy work. If I have not yet finished my course, let me go and speak for thee once more in the fields, seal thy truth, and come home and die." After the sermon, Whitefield traveled to Newburyport, where he lodged at the home of Rev. Jonathan Parsons, pastor of Old South Church. There he spent a restless evening, reading the Bible and Isaac Watts's hymnal. Sleep was in short supply. When asked how he felt, he replied, "I cannot breathe, but I hope I shall be better by and by; a good pulpit sweat today may give me relief; I shall be better after preaching. . . . I had rather wear out than rust out." He had, in fact, worn out in the service of the King of Kings. Before dawn on September 30, 1770, George Whitefield was dead.

Unlike the contemporary world where a person is typically honored by a single funeral or memorial service, while having only one funeral service at Old South Church, Newburyport, Whitefield was honored with dozens of funeral sermons preached by pastors in both North America and England. Rev. Jonathan Parsons of Old South, preaching the day after Whitefield's death, highlighted his contributions to the North American colonies.

> In his repeated visits to America, when his services had almost exhausted his animal spirits, and his friends were ready to cry, "Spare thyself;" his hope of serving Christ, and winning souls to him, animated and engaged him to run almost any risk. Neither did he ever cross the Atlantic, on an itinerating visitation, without visiting his numerous brethren here, to see how religion prospered amongst them; and we know that his labors have been unwearied among us, and to the applause of all his hearers.

Rev. Ebenezer Pemberton of Boston remembered Whitefield's gifts and graces as being "devoted to the honor of

God, and the enlargement of the kingdom of our divine Redeemer." Pemberton reminisced,

> While he preached the gospel, the Holy Ghost was sent down to apply it to the consciences of the hearers; the eyes of the blind were opened, to behold the glories of the compassionate Savior; the ears of the deaf were unstopped, to attend to the invitations of incarnate love; the dead were animated with a divine principle of life; many in all parts of the land were turned from darkness to light, and from the power of Satan unto God. . . . These doctrines . . . seemed to acquire new force, and were attended with uncommon success when delivered by him.

From Northampton, Massachusetts, to Philadelphia, from Charleston to Savannah, fellow pastors reiterated much of what Pemberton and Parsons proclaimed. On the other side of the Atlantic, Henry Venn and John Newton added their voices to what the American clergy valued in Whitefield: his love for the Lord Jesus Christ and his desire to see men, women, and children come to faith in him. But there was another voice yet to be heard: the voice of one whom Whitefield wanted as his eulogist.

When word finally reached England of Whitefield's death, many were surprised at who stepped forward to deliver the primary funeral sermon of the many that were preached on both sides of the Atlantic. John Wesley, whose friendship with Whitefield was severely strained for at least three years, wrote and delivered one of the most eloquent elegies ever delivered for one whose life was dedicated solely to the spread of the gospel of Jesus Christ. Preached from the Tottenham Court Road Tabernacle, where Whitefield intended to be laid to rest, Wesley's sermon was a valiant attempt to celebrate the life and ministry of George Whitefield, highlight the beliefs that he held dear, and minimize the differences that separated Arminian and Calvinistic Methodists from the midpoint of the eighteenth century.

Wesley chose as his text Numbers 23:10: "Let me die the death of the righteous, and let my last end be like his!" It was preached on Sunday, November 18, two months after White-field's death. Wesley outlines the direction his sermon will take: "And may we not, (I) Observe a few particulars of his life and death? (II) Take some view of his character? And, (III) Inquire how we may improve this awful providence, his sudden removal from us?" Wesley delivers on his promise, beginning with a brief, faithful biography of the great evangelist from his inauspicious beginnings in Gloucester, through his conversion during his university years, to the years of international fame, right up to his final moments. One wonders if Wesley's hearers caught the irony as he closed this segment of the message. Whitefield was buried in Newburyport, Massachusetts. Now Wesley was delivering his funeral address over the very spot where Whitefield hoped to be buried.

Wesley continues by outlining the character of his dear friend and colleague. Quoting from an account of Whitefield's character published in Boston since his death, Wesley affirms,

> Little can be said of him, but what every friend to vital Christianity, who has set under his ministry, will attest. In his public labours, he has, for many years, astonished the world with his eloquence and devotion. With what divine pathos did he persuade the impenitent sinner to embrace the practice of piety and virtue! Filled with the Spirit of grace, he spoke from the heart; and, with a fervency of zeal, perhaps unequalled since the days of the apostles, adorned the truths he delivered with the most graceful charms of rhetoric and oratory. From the pulpit he was unrivalled in the command of an ever crowded auditory. Nor was he less agreeable and instructive in his private conversation;—happy in a remarkable ease of address, willing to communicate, studious to edify. May the

rising generation catch a spark of that flame, which shone with such distinguished luster in the spirit and practice of this faithful servant of the Most High God!

Wesley appreciated the generally positive commentary offered by the press in both North America and England, but "they go little farther than the outside of his character. They show you the preacher, but not the man, the Christian, the saint of God." Wesley goes on to provide a more personal, heartfelt assessment of the man he gladly called a "brother in Christ," from "a personal knowledge of near forty years."

Praising the press for their mention of Whitefield's "unparalleled zeal, his indefatigable activity, his tenderheartedness to the afflicted, and charitableness towards the poor," Wesley noted the importance of remembering his "deep gratitude, to all whom God had used as instruments of good to him." He had a deep capacity for friendship; in fact, Wesley goes so far as to suggest that this may have been "the distinguishing part of his character." Whitefield was modest, frank, open, courageous, and steady. And what was the source of his integrity? "It was not the excellence of his natural temper; not the strength of his understanding; it was not the force of education; no, nor the advice of his friends: it was no other than faith in a bleeding Lord; 'faith of the operation of God.' It was 'a lively hope of an inheritance incorruptible, undefiled, and that fadeth not away.'"

Wesley closes this section on Whitefield's character by celebrating that for which the world knew Whitefield: his dynamic giftedness as a preacher.

What an honour it pleased God to put upon his faithful servant, by allowing him to declare his everlasting gospel in so many various countries, to such numbers of people, and with so great an effect on so many of their precious souls! Have we read or heard of any person since the apostles, who testified the gospel of the grace of God through so widely extended a space, through so large a part of the inhabitable world? Have we read or heard of any person, who called so many thousands, so many myriads of sinners to repentance? Above all, have we read or heard of any, who has been a blessed instrument in his hand of bringing so many sinners from "darkness to light, and from the power of Satan unto God?" It is true, were we to talk thus to the gay world, we should be judged to speak as barbarians. But you understand the language of the country to which you are going, and whither our dear friend is gone a little before us.

In the final segment of his sermon, Wesley seeks to make appropriate application to his hearers in light of Whitefield's death. "How shall we improve this awful providence?" Wesley ponders. How can we live in light of his death? The answer, for Wesley, is simple: "By keeping close to the grand doctrines which he delivered; and by drinking into his spirit." Whitefield's fundamental beliefs that his followers must carry were, "Give God all the glory of whatever is good in man, and in the business of salvation, set Christ as high and man as low as possible." While avoiding such theological terms as "free grace" or "election," Wesley has gone as far as he is willing to go to celebrate the doctrines that Whitefield held dear. Some might conclude he was dancing around the issues, some going so far as to attack Wesley the Arminian for daring to preach the funeral sermon for such a dedicated Calvinist. Others may well see it as the generous offering of an "olive branch" to the followers of his departed friend: "Yes, we disagreed on some important theological issues. But the spread of the gospel is more important than theological debate. We agree that people are ruined by sin and stand in need of a Savior and that Jesus is that Savior. Let's work together to make Him known." Wesley celebrates what he describes in Whitefield as possessing a "catholic spirit."

Who is a man of a catholic spirit? One who loves as friends, as brethren in the Lord, as joint partakers of the present kingdom of heaven, and fellow heirs of his eternal kingdom, all, of whatever opinion, mode of worship, or congregation, who believe in the Lord Jesus; who love God and man; who rejoicing to please, and fearing to offend God, are careful to abstain from evil, and zealous of good works. . . . How amiable a character is this!

Wesley did not come to bury Whitefield; that had already taken place in Massachusetts. He came to praise him: his friend and partner in the gospel. Theological debate could wait, and would continue. This was a day to remember a fallen friend and to give thanks to God for the work he accomplished through him.

Perhaps the most poignant written remembrance of Whitefield came from what many might believe to be an unusual source. A native of West Africa, Phillis Wheatley came to America as a slave and was purchased by John Wheatley of Boston as a gift for his wife in 1761. The Wheatleys treated Phillis well, but it is unclear whether she ever received her freedom. In the Wheatley household, Phillis mastered English, along with Latin and Greek, and eventually became the first African-American female poet to publish a book. One of her most famous works is a poem she wrote for Whitefield, himself a slave owner, at the time of his death:

> He prayed that grace in every heart might dwell,
> He longed to see America excel;
> He charg'd its youth to let the grace divine
> Arise, and in their future actions shine.
> He offer'd that he did himself receive,
> A greater gift not God himself can give.
> He urg'd the need of Him to ev'ry one;

It was no less than God's co-equal Son.
Take Him ye wretched for your only good;
Take Him ye starving souls to be your food.
Ye thirsty, come to this life-giving stream;
Ye preachers, take him for your joyful theme.
Take Him, my dear Americans, he said,
Be your complaints in his kind bosom laid.
Take Him, ye Africans, he longs for you;
Impartial Savior is his title due.
If you will choose to walk in grace's road,
You shall be sons, and kings, and priests of God.
Great countess! We Americans revere
Thy name, and thus condole thy grief sincere.
New England, sure doth feel; the orphan's smart
Reveals the true sensations of his heart.
His lonely Tabernacle sees no more
A Whitefield landing on the British shore.
Then let us view him in your azure skies,
Let every mind with this lov'd object rise.
Thou tomb, shall safe retain thy sacred trust,
Till life divine re-animates his dust.

Whitefield's legacy lived on in both thoughtful remembrances and in ways that can only be described as odd. His burial site became a major destination for a Protestant form of pilgrimage. The faithful came to visit the crypt that was originally located just beneath the pulpit of Old South Church. In an age when the public had more access to such sites, it was common occurrence for visitors to actually lift the lid of the coffin and inspect Whitefield's earthly remains. One such visitor, Jesse Lee, one of the early leaders of late-eighteenth century American Methodism, tells of his macabre visit to Whitefield's tomb after removing the lid of the coffin:

[We] beheld the awful ravages of "the last enemy of man."
How quiet the repose, how changed the features of the man

whose impassioned eloquence had moved multitudes to tears of penitence, and the impulses of a new-born zeal for God! His face had lost its comeliness, the fire of his eye was extinct, and he lay like a mighty warrior quietly reposing after the strife of conquest and the shout of victory. Death was gradually reducing his corporeal substance to its primitive dust.

Abel Stevens, another American Methodist, also made the pilgrimage to Newburyport as part of his research for writing his history of Methodism. He descended beneath the pulpit with his guide and found that "the bare and decaying bones lie upon a slight bed of mold formed of the dust of the body. As the thoughtful spectator gazes upon the fully-formed cranium, or takes it into his hands, many an eager inquiry is startled within him. What thoughts and power of grandeur emanated from this dome of the mind, thoughts that have stirred the depths of hundreds of thousands of souls, and will quicken their immortality!"

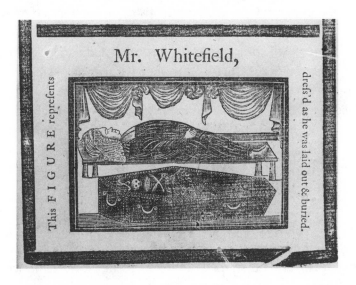

6.2 Whitefield's early death at age 55 helped to fuel popular superstitions about him. His burial site in Newburyport, Massachusetts, became a place of pilgrimage and plunder.

Other unusual memorials sprung up over the years. Worshipers at the Tottenham Court Road Tabernacle were surprised at one service to find a young preacher who "looked somewhat like Mr. Whitefield in the face." In Boston, a wax figure of Whitefield was crafted that "amazed spectators of all ranks." Perhaps upset that Whitefield, a native of England, was buried in North America, someone actually stole one of his arm bones and whisked it off to England. It remained in England until 1849 when it came into possession of a friend and admirer of the Grand Itinerant. He returned it to Old South Church in a small wooden box now on display in the church's vestibule. A few hundred miles south of Newburyport in Madison, New Jersey, the archives of the United Methodist Church on the campus of Drew University reportedly have one of the mummified thumbs of George Whitefield. No one is sure how it got there.

Memorials of a less strange and more lasting kind represent the legacy George Whitefield left to the church of all ages. A key component of that legacy is that Whitefield understood the power of contemporary media in spreading the gospel of Jesus Christ. By twenty-first century standards, the media outlets available to Whitefield were few and far between. But Whitefield made the optimal use of those to which he had access. The primary means of disseminating ideas in Whitefield's day was through the press. Not only did Whitefield publish his journals and sermons, but he used England's and America's newspapers to announce upcoming preaching dates, publish sermons, and even attract attention to the message through controversy. Whitefield sold newspapers, so he could count on the editors of newspapers up and down the East Coast of the North American colonies and throughout the British Isles to keep spreading the news of the revival. They spread the news of the revivals.

The people came to hear Whitefield. Whitefield shared the good news of salvation. God gave the increase.

Over the course of the last 250 years, many successful Christian ministries have followed Whitefield's example of using the contemporary media to share God's good news. Since the early days of radio and television, evangelicals have captured the potential those technologies presented for the spread of the gospel. Satellite technology, personal computers, and the Internet have opened new doors for the furtherance of the message of Christianity, and many organizations, from local churches to seminaries, from mission organizations to Bible translators, are capturing the power and the potential that these hold for letting "the whole world know" about Jesus.

Whitefield also left to the church the example of field preaching, which in reality was an early form of the type of evangelism practiced by such Christian leaders as Dwight L. Moody, Billy Sunday, and Billy Graham. Sometimes labeled, rather unfortunately, "crusade" evangelism, it was a pattern set by Whitefield for many itinerant evangelists, and it has lasted into the twenty-first century. His model was simple: preach to as many people as you can in the largest convenient location you can. No doubt many went to a Whitefield meeting simply to find out what all the commotion was about, or because they had nothing better to do. But God used those events, no matter what the hearers' motives might have been for attending, in order to lead countless individuals to the foot of the cross of Christ. The crowds that Whitefield drew pale in comparison to those attracted to evangelistic events on football fields and in baseball stadiums, but he left a pattern that many have copied for nearly three hundred years.

A tangible piece of Whitefield's legacy in America stands just outside the city of Savannah, Georgia. The orphan house that Whitefield established on the model of the Pietist orphanage in Halle, Germany, still exists today, although it has evolved into a slightly different ministry. Still dedicated to Whitefield's guiding principles of "a love of God; a love of learning, and a strong work ethic," Bethesda Academy is a private residential and day school for young men in grades six through twelve. It provides a strong academic program, coupled with regular attention to the spiritual development of the students and job training as they approach graduation. The chapel on the campus is dedicated to Whitefield's memory. In fact, a walking tour of the historic district of Savannah will remind visitors of the positive contributions he made to the city. One of the city's beautiful squares bears his name. The beautiful edifice of Christ Episcopal Church holds two plaques in memory of the two brothers in Christ whose pastoral ministry led to the founding of Christ Church: John Wesley and George Whitefield.

Arguably the greatest legacy that George Whitefield left to the church was his commitment to the preaching of the Word of God. Zwingli, Calvin, Cranmer, and other leaders of the Protestant Reformation during the sixteenth century recaptured the fire and force of biblical preaching. Even when some of that fire was lost within the Church of England, and sermons became little more than lessons in being a gentleman, Puritans and other Dissenters stayed true to the exposition of the Scriptures as the centerpiece of worship. George Whitefield revolutionized biblical preaching for the Church of England and the church universal. Using the principles he had discovered as a child acting in school plays, Whitefield adopted them for preaching the Word of God. Benjamin Franklin commented,

> By hearing him often, I came to distinguish easily between sermons newly compos'd, and those which he had often

preach'd in the course of his travels. His delivery of the latter was so improv'd by frequent repetitions that every accent, every emphasis, every modulation of his voice, was so perfectly well turn'd and well plac'd, that, without being interested in the subject, one could not help being pleas'd with the discourse; a pleasure of much the same kind with that receiv'd from an excellent piece of musick.

What made Whitefield different from so many of his contemporaries was that he employed his dramatic gifts as a means of preaching the Word. What made Whitefield different from so many of today's popular preachers is that he never allowed the dramatic to overshadow the Word.

Old South Presbyterian Church is still a worshiping community of faith in the city of Newburyport, Massachusetts. With a phone call or e-mail, visitors can secure a guided tour of this grand historic church in a picturesque New England coastal town. Guests will be entertained with stories of the daring theft of the Bird of Dawning weather vane from the top of the bell tower. Visitors will marvel at the acoustics of the Whispering Gallery and be saddened by the presence of slave pews—a reminder of a sordid page from our American history. With the right tour guide, the daring might even venture to the heights of Old South—right into the bell tower—and see etched in the bell the name "P. Revere." It is one of only a handful of bells cast by Paul Revere still rung every Sunday morning.

Visitors will also be guided around the back of the pulpit and down the stairs to the final resting place of George Whitefield. Over thirty thousand people have visited since 1770: some out of curiosity; some, no doubt, due to the bizarre stories of tomb-raiding colonials. Some come to recapture some of the emotion captured by American poet John Greenleaf Whittier in his poem "The Preacher."

Long shall the traveler strain his eye
From the railroad car as it plunges by,
And the vanishing town behind him search
For the slender spire of the Whitefield Church,
And feel for one moment the ghosts of trade,
And fashion and folly and pleasure laid,
By the thought of that life of pure intent,
That voice of warning yet eloquent,
Of one on the errands of angels sent.

And if, where he labored, the flood of sin,
Like a tide from the harbor bar sets in,
And over a life of time and sense
The church spires lift their vain defence.
. . . .
Still, as the gem of its civic crown,
Precious beyond the world's renown,
His memory hallows the ancient town.

But others come to recapture something they know is missing from the churches they attend and the cultures in which they live. The bold witness. The one who proclaims truth, no matter who might be offended. The fearless prophet. The Grand Itinerant. A powerful preacher of God's redeeming grace like George Whitefield.

PART TWO

THE GRAND ITINERANT IN PRINT

7

Excerpts from the Writings of George Whitefield

As a young preacher, George Whitefield took that rather audacious step of publishing an account of his early life and ministry. Whitefield gives his readers an important look into his childhood, his early education, and his conversion, but many detractors felt he was too young and too inexperienced to be publishing such an account. He later issued an edited version, with much of the self-aggrandizing material removed. The first edition, from which this excerpt is extracted, was first published in 1738. Parts that Whitefield removed for the 1756 edition are enclosed in brackets. As far as possible, Whitefield's spelling and grammar have been retained.

I was born in Gloucester, in the month of December, 1714. [My father and mother kept the Bell Inn. The former died when I was two years old; the latter is now alive, and has often told me how she endured fourteen weeks' sickness after she brought me into the world; but was used to say, even when I was an infant, that she expected more comfort from me than any other of her children. This, with the circumstances of my being born in an inn, has been often of service to me in exciting my endeavors to make good my mother's expectations, and so follow the example of my dear Saviour, who was born in a manger belonging to an inn.

My very infant years must necessarily not be mentioned; yet I can remember such early stirrings of corruption in my heart, as abundantly convinces me that I was conceived and born in sin; that in me dwelleth no good thing by nature, and that if God had not freely prevented me by His grace, I must have been for ever banished from His Divine presence.]

I can truly say I was froward from my mother's womb. I was so brutish as to hate instruction, and used purposely to shun opportunities of receiving it. I can date some very early acts of uncleanness. [I soon gave pregnant proofs of an impudent temper.] Lying, filthy talking, and foolish jesting I was much addicted to[, even when very young]. Sometimes I used to curse, if not swear. Stealing from my mother I thought no theft at all, and used to make no scruple of taking money out of her pocket before she was up. I have frequently betrayed my trust, and have more than once spent money I took in the house, in buying fruits, tarts, etc., to satisfy my sensual appetite. Numbers of Sabbaths have I broken, and generally used to behave myself very irreverently in God's sanctuary. Much money have I spent in plays, and in the common entertainments of the age. Cards, and reading romances, were my heart's delight. Often have I joined with others in playing roguish tricks, but was generally, if not always, happily detected. For this, I have often since, and do now bless and praise God. . . .

During the time of my being at school, I was very fond of reading plays, and have kept from school for days together to prepare myself for acting them. My master seeing how mine and my schoolfellows' vein ran, composed something of this kind for us himself, and caused me to dress myself in girls' clothes, which I had often done, to act a part before the corporation. The remembrance of this has often covered me with confusion of face, and I hope will do so, even to the end of my life. . . .

[One morning, as I was reading a play to my sister, said I, "Sister, God intends something for me which we know not of. As I have been diligent in business, I believe many would gladly have me for an apprentice, but every way seems to be barred up, so that I think God will provide for me some way or other that we cannot apprehend."

How I came to say these words I know not. God afterwards showed me they came from Him.] Having thus lived with my mother for some considerable time, a young student, who was once my schoolfellow, and then a servitor of Pembroke College, Oxford, came to pay my mother a visit. Amongst other conversation, he told her how he had discharged all college expenses that quarter, and received a penny. Upon that my mother immediately cried out, "This will do for my son." Then turning to me, she said, "Will you go to Oxford, George?" I replied, "With all my heart." Whereupon, having the same friends that this young student had, my mother, without delay, waited on them. They promised their interest to get me a servitor's place in the same college. She then applied to my old master, who much approved of my coming to school again. . . .

I now[1] began to pray and sing psalms thrice every day, besides morning and evening, and to fast every Friday, and to receive the Sacrament at a parish church near our college, and at the castle, where the despised Methodists used to receive once a month.

The young men so called were then much talked of at Oxford. I had heard of, and loved them before I came to the University; and so strenuously defended them when I heard them reviled by the students, that they began to think that I also in time should be one of them.

For above twelvemonth my soul longed to be acquainted with some of them, and I was strongly pressed to follow their

1. From this paragraph onward, Whitefield is describing his time at Oxford.

good example, when I saw them go through a ridiculing crowd to receive the Holy Eucharist at St. Mary's. At length, God was pleased to open a door. It happened that a poor woman in one of the workhouses had attempted to cut her throat, but was happily prevented. Upon hearing of this, and knowing that both the Mr. Wesleys were ready to every good work, I sent a poor apple-woman of our college to inform Mr. Charles Wesley of it, charging her not to discover who sent her. She went; but, contrary to my orders, told my name. He having heard of my coming to the castle and a parish-church sacrament, and having met me frequently walking by myself, followed the woman when she was gone away, and sent an invitation to me by her, to come to breakfast with him the next morning.

I thankfully embraced the opportunity; [and, blessed be God! it was one of the most profitable visits I ever made in my life. My soul, at that time, was athirst for some spiritual friends to lift up my hands when they hung down, and to strengthen my feeble knees. He soon discovered it, and, like a wise winner of souls, made all his discourses tend that way. And when he had] put into my hands Professor Francke's treatise *Against the Fear of Man*[, and a book, entitled, *The Country Parson's Advice to His Parishioners* (the last of which was wonderfully blessed to my soul) I took my leave].

In a short time he let me have another book, entitled, *The Life of God in the Soul of Man*[; and, though I had fasted, watched and prayed, and received the Sacrament so long, yet I never knew what true religion was, till God sent me that excellent treatise by the hands of my never-to-be-forgotten friend].

At my first reading it, I wondered what the author meant by saying, "That some falsely placed religion in going to church, doing hurt to no one, being constant in the duties of the closet, and now and then reaching out their hands to give alms to their poor neighbors." "Alas!" thought I, "if this be not true religion, what is?" God soon showed me;

for in reading a few lines further, that "true religion was union of the soul with God, and Christ formed within us," a ray of Divine light was instantaneously darted in upon my soul, and from that moment, but not till then, did I know that I must be a new creature."

Beginning in 1739 and lasting until 1741, the friendship of George Whitefield and John Wesley was seriously strained, at least in part by Wesley's decision to "preach and print" his sermon titled, "Free Grace." In response, Whitefield pens a letter refuting Wesley's sermon point by point. It is included here to give the reader insight into Whitefield's Reformed theology and his desire to "rightly divide the Word of truth." Fortunately for the sake of the revivals, the two friends reconciled, agreed to disagree, and spent the remainder of their lives minimizing their differences and concentrating their efforts on the proclamation of the gospel. (From this point forward, brackets are used in the typical way—to indicate material that has been added to Whitefield's original text.)

A LETTER FROM GEORGE WHITEFIELD TO THE REV. MR. JOHN WESLEY IN ANSWER TO MR. WESLEY'S SERMON ENTITLED "FREE GRACE"

"But when Peter was come to Antioch, I withstood him to the face, because he was to be blamed." (Gal. 2:11)

Preface

I am very well aware what different effects publishing this letter against the dear Mr. Wesley's Sermon will produce. Many of my friends who are strenuous advocates for *universal redemption* will immediately be offended. Many who are zealous on the other side will be much rejoiced. They who are lukewarm on both sides and are carried away with carnal reasoning will wish this matter had never been brought under debate.

The reasons I have given at the beginning of the letter, I think are sufficient to satisfy all of my conduct herein. I desire therefore that they who hold election would not triumph, or make a party on one hand (for I detest any such thing)—and that they who are prejudiced against that doctrine be not too much concerned or offended on the other.

Known unto God are all his ways from the beginning of the world. The great day will discover why the Lord permits dear Mr. Wesley and me to be of a different way of thinking. At present, I shall make no enquiry into that matter, beyond the account which he has given of it himself in the following letter, which I lately received from his own dear hands:

London, August 9, 1740

My dear Brother,

I thank you for yours, May the 24th. The case is quite plain. There are bigots both for predestination and against it. God is sending a message to those on either side. But neither will receive it, unless from one who is of their own opinion. Therefore, for a time you are suffered to be of one opinion, and I of another. But when his time is come, God will do what man cannot, namely, make us both of one mind. Then persecution will flame out, and it will be seen whether we count our lives dear unto ourselves, so that we may finish our course with joy. I am, my dearest brother,

Ever yours,

J. WESLEY

Thus my honoured friend, I heartily pray God to hasten the time, for his being clearly enlightened into all the doctrines of divine revelation, that we may thus be closely united in principle and judgment as well as heart and affection. And then if the Lord should call us to it, I care not if I go with him to prison, or to death. For like Paul and Silas, I hope we shall sing praises to God, and count it our highest honour to suffer for Christ's sake, and to lay down our lives for the brethren.

Whitefield's Letter to Wesley

Bethesda in Georgia, Dec. 24, 1740

Reverend and very dear Brother,

God only knows what unspeakable sorrow of heart I have felt on your account since I left England last. Whether it be my infirmity or not, I frankly confess, that Jonah could not go with more reluctance against Nineveh, than I now take pen in hand to write against you. Was nature to speak, I had rather die than do it; and yet if I am faithful to God, and to my own and others' souls, I must not stand neutral any longer. I am very apprehensive that our common adversaries will rejoice to see us differing among ourselves. But what can I say? The children of God are in danger of falling into error. Nay, numbers *have* been misled, whom God has been pleased to work upon by my ministry, and a greater number are still calling aloud upon me to show also my opinion. I must then show that I know no man after the flesh, and that I have no respect to persons, any further than is consistent with my duty to my Lord and Master, *Jesus Christ*.

This letter, no doubt, will lose me many friends: and for this cause perhaps God has laid this difficult task upon me, even to see whether I am willing to forsake all for him, or not. From such considerations as these, I think it my duty to bear an humble testimony, and earnestly to plead for the truths which, I am convinced, are clearly revealed in the Word of God. In the defence whereof I must use great plainness of speech, and treat my dearest friends upon earth with the greatest simplicity, faithfulness, and freedom, leaving the consequences of all to God.

For some time before, and especially since my last departure from England, both in public and private, by preaching and printing, you have been propagating the doctrine of *universal redemption*. And when I remember how Paul reproved Peter for his dissimulation, I fear I have been sinfully silent too long. O then be not angry with me, dear and honoured Sir, if now I deliver my soul, by telling you that I think in this you greatly err.

'Tis not my design to enter into a long debate on God's decrees. I refer you to Dr. Edwards his *Veritas Redux*, which, I think is unanswerable—except in a certain point, concerning a *middle sort* between elect and reprobate, which he himself in effect afterwards condemns.

I shall only make a few remarks upon your sermon, entitled *Free Grace*. And before I enter upon the discourse itself, give me leave to take a little notice of what in your Preface you term an indispensable obligation to make it public to all the world. I must own, that I always thought you were quite mistaken upon that head.

The case (you know) stands thus: When you were at Bristol, I think you received a letter from a private hand, charging you with not preaching the gospel, because you did not preach up election. Upon this you drew a lot: the answer was "*preach and print.*" I have often questioned, as I do now, whether in so doing, you did not tempt the Lord. A due exercise of religious prudence, without [the drawing of] a lot, would have directed you in that matter. Besides, I never heard that you enquired of God, whether or not election was a gospel doctrine.

But, I fear, taking it for granted [that election was not a biblical truth], you only enquired whether you should be silent or preach and print against it.

However this be, the lot came out *"preach and print"*; accordingly you preached and printed against election. At my desire, you suppressed the publishing of the sermon whilst I was in England; but you soon sent it into the world after my departure. O that you had kept it in! However, if that sermon was printed in answer to a lot, I am apt to think, one reason why God should so suffer you to be deceived, was, that hereby a special obligation might be laid upon me, faithfully to declare the Scripture doctrine of election, that thus the Lord might give me a fresh opportunity of seeing what was in my heart, and whether I would be true to his cause or not; as you could not but grant, he did once before, by giving you such another lot at Deal.

The morning I sailed from Deal for Gibraltar [February 2, 1738], you arrived from Georgia. Instead of giving me an opportunity to converse with you, though the ship was not far off the shore, you drew a lot, and immediately set forward to London. You left a letter behind you, in which were words to this effect: "When I saw [that] God, by the wind which was carrying you out, brought me in, I asked counsel of God. His answer you have enclosed." This was a piece of paper, in which were written these words, "Let him return to London."

When I received this, I was somewhat surprised. Here was a good man telling me he had cast a lot, and that God would have me return to London. On the other hand, I knew my call was to Georgia, and that I had taken leave of London, and could not justly go from the soldiers, who were committed to my charge. I betook myself with a friend to prayer. That passage in 1 Kings 13 was powerfully impressed upon my soul, where we are told that the Prophet was slain by a lion when he was tempted to go back (contrary to God's express orders) upon another Prophet's telling him God would have him do so. I wrote you word that I could not return to London. We sailed immediately.

Some months after, I received a letter from you at Georgia, wherein you wrote words to this effect: "Though God never before gave me a wrong lot, yet, perhaps, he suffered me to have such a lot at that time, to try what was in your heart." I should never have published this private transaction to the world, did not the glory of God call me to it. It is plain you had a wrong lot given you here, and justly, because you tempted God in drawing one. And thus I believe it is in the present case. And if so, let not the children of God who are mine and your intimate friends, and also advocates for *universal redemption*, think that doctrine true—because you preached it up in compliance with a lot given out from God.

This, I think, may serve as an answer to that part of the Preface to your printed sermon, wherein you say, "Nothing but the strongest conviction, not only that what is here advanced is the truth as it is in Jesus, but also that I am indispensably obliged to declare this truth to all the world." That you believe what you have written to be truth, and that you honestly aim at God's glory in writing, I do not in the least doubt. But then, honoured Sir, I cannot but think you have been much mistaken in imagining that your tempting God, by casting a lot in the manner you did could lay you under an *indispensable obligation* to any action, much less to publish your sermon against the doctrine of *predestination to life*.

I must next observe, that as you have been unhappy in printing at all upon such an *imaginary warrant*, so you have been as unhappy in the choice of your text. Honoured Sir, how could it enter into your heart to choose a text to disprove the doctrine of election out of the eighth of Romans, where this doctrine is so plainly asserted? Once I spoke with a Quaker upon this subject, and he had no other way of evading the force of the Apostle's assertion than by saying, "I believe Paul was in the wrong." And another friend lately, who was once highly prejudiced against election, ingenuously confessed that he used to think St. Paul himself was mistaken, or that he was not truly translated.

Indeed, honoured Sir, it is plain beyond all contradiction that St. Paul, through the whole of Romans 8, is speaking of the privileges of those only who are really in Christ. And let any unprejudiced person read what goes before and what follows your text, and he must confess the word "all" only signifies those that are in Christ. And the latter part of the text plainly proves, what, I find, dear Mr. Wesley will, by no means, grant. I mean the *final perseverance* of the children of God: "He that spared not his own Son, but delivered him up for us all (*i.e.*, all Saints), how shall he not with him also freely give us all things?" [Rom. 8:32]. [He shall give us] grace, in particular, to enable us to persevere, and every thing else necessary to carry us home to our Father's heavenly kingdom.

Had any one a mind to prove the doctrine of *election*, as well as of *final perseverance*, he could hardly wish for a text more fit for his purpose than that which you have chosen to disprove it! One who did not know you would suspect that you were aware of this, for after the first paragraph, I scarce know whether you have mentioned [the text] so much as once through your whole sermon.

But your discourse, in my opinion, is as little to the purpose as your text, and instead of warping, does but more and more confirm me in the belief of the doctrine of God's *eternal election*.

I shall not mention how illogically you have proceeded. Had you written clearly, you should first, honoured Sir, have proved your proposition: "God's grace is free to all." And then by way of inference [you might have] exclaimed against what you call *the horrible decree*. But you knew that people (because *Arminianism*, of late, has so much abounded among us) were generally prejudiced against the doctrine of *reprobation*, and therefore thought if you kept up their dislike of that, you could overthrow the doctrine of election entirely. For, without doubt, the doctrine of election and reprobation must stand or fall together.

But passing by this, as also your equivocal definition of the word *grace*, and your false definition of the word *free*, and that I may be as short as possible, I frankly acknowledge, I believe the doctrine of reprobation, in this view, that God intends to give saving grace, through Jesus Christ, only to a certain number, and that the rest of mankind, after the fall of Adam, being justly left of God to continue in sin, will at last suffer that eternal death, which is its proper wages.

This is the established doctrine of Scripture, and acknowledged as such in the 17th article of the Church of England, as Bishop Burnet himself confesses. Yet dear Mr. Wesley absolutely denies it.

But the most important objections you have urged against this doctrine as reasons why you reject it, being seriously considered, and faithfully tried by the Word of God, will appear to be of no force at all. Let the matter be humbly and calmly reviewed, as to the following heads:

First, you say that if this be so (*i.e.*, if there be an election) then is all preaching vain: it is needless to them that are elected; for they, whether with preaching or without, will infallibly be saved. Therefore, the end of preaching to save souls is void with regard to them. And it is useless to them that are not elected, for they cannot possibly be saved. They, whether with preaching or without, will infallibly be damned. The end of preaching is therefore void with regard to them likewise. So that in either case our preaching is vain, and your hearing also vain.

O dear Sir, what kind of reasoning—or rather sophistry—is this! Hath not God, who hath appointed salvation for a certain number, appointed also the preaching of the Word as a means to bring them to it? Does anyone hold election in any other sense? And if so, how is preaching needless to them that are elected, when the gospel is designated by God himself to be the power of God unto their eternal salvation? And since we know not who are elect and who reprobate, we are to preach promiscuously to all. For the Word may be useful, even to the non-elect, in restraining them from much wickedness and sin. However, it is enough to excite to the utmost diligence in preaching and hearing, when we consider that by these means, some, even as many as the Lord hath ordained to eternal life, shall certainly be quickened and enabled to believe. And who that attends, especially with reverence and care, can tell but he may be found of that happy number?

Second, you say that the doctrine of election and reprobation directly tends to destroy that holiness which is the end of all the ordinances of God. For (says the dear mistaken Mr. Wesley) "it wholly takes away those first motives to follow after it, so frequently proposed in Scripture. The hope of future reward, and fear of punishment, the hope of heaven, and the fear of hell, et cetera."

I thought that one who carries perfection to such an exalted pitch as dear Mr. Wesley does would know, that a true lover of the Lord Jesus Christ would strive to be holy for the sake of being holy, and work for Christ out of love and gratitude, without any regard to the rewards of heaven, or fear of hell. You remember, dear Sir, what Scougal says, "Love's a more powerful motive that does them move." But passing by this, and granting that rewards and punishments (as they certainly are) may be motives from which a Christian may be honestly stirred up to act for God, how does the doctrine of election destroy these motives? Do not the elect know that the more good works they do, the greater will be their reward? And is not that encouragement enough to set them upon, and cause them to persevere in working for Jesus Christ? And how does the doctrine of election destroy holiness? Who ever preached any other election than what the Apostle preached, when he said, "Chosen . . . through sanctification of the Spirit" [2 Thess. 2:13]? Nay, is not holiness made a mark of our election by all that preach it? And how then can the doctrine of election destroy holiness?

The instance which you bring to illustrate your assertion, indeed, dear Sir, is quite impertinent. For you say, "If a sick man knows that he must unavoidably die or unavoidably recover, though he knows not which, it is not reasonable to take any physic at all." Dear Sir, what absurd reasoning is here? Were you ever sick in your life? If so, did not the bare probability or possibility of your recovering, though you knew it was unalterably fixed that you must live or die, encourage you to take physic? For how did you know but that very physic might be the means God intended to recover you by?

Just thus it is as to the doctrine of election. I know that it is unalterably fixed (one may say) that I must be damned or saved; but since I know not which for a certainty, why should I not strive, though at present in a state of nature, since I know not but this striving may be the means God has intended to bless, in order to bring me into a state of grace?

Dear Sir, consider these things. Make an impartial application, and then judge what little reason you had to conclude the 10th paragraph, page 12, with these words: "So directly does this doctrine tend to shut the very gate of holiness in general, to hinder unholy men from ever approaching thereto, or striving to enter in thereat."

"As directly," you say, "does the doctrine tend to destroy several particular branches of holiness, such as meekness, love, et cetera." I shall say little, dear Sir, in answer to this paragraph. Dear Mr. Wesley perhaps has been disputing with some warm narrow-spirited men that held election, and then he infers that their warmth and narrowness of spirit was owing to their principles? But does not dear Mr. Wesley know many dear children of God, who are predestinarians, and yet are meek, lowly, pitiful, courteous, tender-hearted, kind, of a catholic spirit, and hope to see the most vile and profligate of men converted? And why? Because they know God saved themselves by an act of his electing love, and they know not but he may have elected those who now seem to be the most abandoned.

But, dear Sir, we must not judge of the truth of principles in general, nor of this of election in particular, entirely from the practice of some that profess to hold them. If so, I am sure much might be said against your own. For I appeal to your own heart, whether or not you have not felt in yourself, or observed in others, a narrow-spiritedness, and some disunion of soul respecting those that hold *universal redemption*. If so, then according to your own rule, *universal redemption* is *wrong*, because it destroys several branches of holiness, such as meekness, love, et cetera. But not to insist upon this, I beg you would observe that your inference is entirely set aside by the force of the Apostle's argument, and the language which he expressly uses in Colossians 3:12–13: "Put on therefore, as the elect of God, holy and beloved, bowels of mercies, kindness, humbleness of mind, meekness, longsuffering; forbearing one another, and forgiving one another, if any man have a quarrel against any: even as Christ forgave you, so also do ye."

Here we see that the Apostle exhorts them to put on bowels of mercy, kindness, humbleness of mind, meekness, long-suffering, et cetera, upon this consideration: namely, because they were elect of God. And all who have experientially felt this doctrine in their hearts feel that these graces are the genuine effects of their being elected of God.

But perhaps dear Mr. Wesley may be mistaken in this point, and call that passion which is only zeal for God's truths. You know, dear Sir, the Apostle exhorts us to "contend earnestly for the faith once delivered to the saints" [Jude 3]. Therefore you must not condemn all that appear zealous for the doctrine of election as narrow-spirited, or persecutors, just because they think it their duty to oppose you. I am sure, I love you in the bowels of Jesus Christ, and think I could lay down my life for your sake; but yet, dear Sir, I cannot help strenuously opposing your errors upon this important subject, because I think you warmly, though not designedly, oppose the truth, as it is in Jesus. May the Lord remove the scales of prejudice from off the eyes of your mind and give you a zeal according to true Christian knowledge!

Third, says your sermon, "This doctrine tends to destroy the comforts of religion, the happiness of Christianity, et cetera."

But how does Mr. Wesley know this, who never believed election? I believe they who have experienced it will agree with our 17th article, that "the godly consideration of predestination, and election in Christ, is full of sweet, pleasant, unspeakable comfort to godly persons, and such as feel in themselves the working of the Spirit of Christ, mortifying the works of the flesh, and their earthly members, and drawing their minds to high and heavenly things, as well because it does greatly establish and confirm their faith of eternal salvation, to be enjoyed through Christ, as because it doth fervently kindle their love towards God," et cetera.

This plainly shows that our godly reformers did not think election destroyed holiness or the comforts of religion. As for my own part, this doctrine is my daily support. I should utterly sink under a dread of my impending trials, were I not firmly persuaded that God has chosen me in Christ from before the foundation of the world, and that now being effectually called, he will allow no one to pluck me out of his almighty hand.

You proceed thus: "This is evident as to all those who believe themselves to be reprobate, or only suspect or fear it; all the great and precious promises are lost to them; they afford them no ray of comfort."

In answer to this, let me observe that none living, especially none who are desirous of salvation, can know that they are not of the number of God's elect. None but the unconverted, can have any just reason so much as to fear it. And would dear Mr. Wesley give comfort, or dare you apply the precious promises of the gospel, being children's bread, to men in a natural state, while they continue so? God forbid! What if the doctrine of election and reprobation *does* put some upon doubting? So does that of regeneration. But, is not this doubting a good means to put them upon searching and striving; and that striving, a good means to make their calling and their election sure?

This is one reason among many others why I admire the doctrine of election and am convinced that it should have a place in gospel ministrations and should be insisted on with faithfulness and care. It has a natural tendency to rouse the soul out of its carnal security. And therefore many carnal men cry out against it. Whereas universal redemption is a notion sadly adapted to keep the soul in its lethargic sleepy condition, and therefore so many natural men admire and applaud it.

Your 13th, 14th and 15th paragraphs come next to be considered. "The witness of the Spirit," you say, "experience shows to be much obstructed by this doctrine."

But, dear Sir, whose experience? Not your own; for in your journal, from your embarking for Georgia, to your return to London, you seem to acknowledge that you have it not, and therefore you are no competent judge in this matter. You must mean then the experience of others. For you say in the same paragraph, "Even in those who have tasted of that good gift, who yet have soon lost it again," (I suppose you mean lost the sense of it again) "and fallen back into doubts and fears and darkness, even horrible darkness that might be felt, et cetera." Now, as to the darkness of desertion, was not this the case of Jesus Christ himself, after he had received an unmeasurable unction of the Holy Ghost? Was not his soul exceeding sorrowful, even unto death, in the garden? And was he not surrounded with an horrible darkness, even a darkness that might be felt, when on the cross he cried out, "My God! My God! why hast thou forsaken me?"

And that all his followers are liable to the same, is it not evident from Scripture? For, says the Apostle, "He was tempted in all things like as we are," [Heb. 4:15] "so that he himself might be able to succour those that are tempted" [Heb. 2:18]. And is not their liableness thereunto consistent with that conformity to him in suffering, which his members are to bear [Phil. 3:10]? Why then should persons falling into darkness, after they have received the witness of the Spirit, be any argument against the doctrine of election?

"Yes," you say, "many, very many of those that hold it not, in all parts of the earth, have enjoyed the uninterrupted witness of the Spirit, the continual light of God's countenance, from the moment wherein they first believed, for many months or years, to this very day." But how does dear Mr. Wesley know this? Has he consulted the experience of many, very many in all parts of the earth? Or could he be sure of what he hath advanced without sufficient grounds, would it follow that their being kept in this light is owing to their not believing the doctrine of election? No, this [doctrine], according to the sentiments of our church, "greatly confirms and establishes a true Christian's faith of eternal salvation through Christ," and is an anchor of hope, both sure and steadfast, when he walks in darkness and sees no light; as certainly he may, even after he hath received the witness of the Spirit, whatever you or others may unadvisedly assert to the contrary.

Then, to have respect to God's everlasting covenant, and to throw himself upon the free distinguishing love of that God who changeth not, will make him lift up the hands that hang down, and strengthen the feeble knees.

But without the belief of the doctrine of election, and the immutability of the free love of God, I cannot see how it is possible that any should have a comfortable assurance of eternal salvation. What could it signify to a man whose conscience is thoroughly awakened, and who is warned in good earnest to seek deliverance from the wrath to come, though he should be assured that all his past sins be forgiven, and that he is now a child of God; if notwithstanding this, he may hereafter become a child of the devil, and be cast into hell at last? Could such an assurance yield any solid, lasting comfort to a person convinced of the corruption and treachery of his own heart, and of the malice, subtlety, and power of Satan? No! That which alone deserves the name of a full assurance of faith is such an assurance as emboldens the believer, under the sense of his interest in distinguishing love, to give the challenge to all his adversaries, whether men or devils, and that with regard to all their future, as well as present, attempts to destroy—saying with the Apostle, "Who shall lay any thing to the charge of God's elect? It is God that justifieth. Who is he that condemneth? It is Christ that died, yea rather, that is risen again, who is even at the right hand of God, who also maketh intercession for us. Who shall separate us from the love of Christ? Shall tribulation, or distress, or persecution, or famine, or nakedness, or peril, or sword? As it is written, For thy sake we are killed all the day long; we are accounted as sheep for the slaughter. Nay, in all these things we are more than conquerors through him that loved us. For I am persuaded, that neither death, nor life, nor angels, nor principalities, nor powers, nor things present, nor things to come, nor height, nor depth, nor any other creature, shall be able to separate us from the love of God, which is in Christ Jesus our Lord" [Rom. 8:33–39]. This, dear Sir, is the triumphant language of every soul that has attained a full assurance of faith. And this assurance can only arise from a belief of God's electing everlasting love. That many have an assurance they are in Christ today, but take no thought for, or are not assured they shall be in him tomorrow—nay to all eternity—is rather their imperfection and unhappiness than their privilege. I pray God to bring all such to a sense of his eternal love, that they may no longer build upon their own faithfulness, but on the unchangeableness of that God whose gifts and callings are without repentance. For those whom God has once justified, he also will glorify.

I observed before, dear Sir, it is not always a safe rule to judge of the truth of principles from people's practice. And therefore, supposing that all who hold *universal redemption* in your way of explaining it, after they received faith, enjoyed the continual uninterrupted sight of God's countenance, it does not follow that this is a fruit of their principle. For that I am sure has a natural tendency to keep the soul in darkness for ever, because the creature thereby is taught that his being kept in a state of salvation is owing to his own free will. And what a sandy foundation is that for a poor creature to build his hopes of perseverance upon? Every relapse into sin, every surprise by temptation, must throw him "into doubts and fears, into horrible darkness, even darkness that may be felt."

Hence it is that the letters which have been lately sent me by those who hold universal redemption are dead and life-less, dry and inconsistent, in comparison of those I receive from persons on the contrary side. Those who settle in the universal scheme, though they might begin in the Spirit, (whatever they may say to the contrary) are ending in the flesh, and building up a righteousness founded on their own free will: whilst the others triumph in hope of the glory of God, and build upon God's never-failing promise and unchangeable love, even when his sensible presence is with-drawn from them.

But I would not judge of the truth of election by the experience of any particular persons: if I did (O bear with me in this foolishness of boasting) I think I myself might glory in election. For these five or six years I have received the witness of God's Spirit; since that, blessed be God, I have not doubted a quarter of an hour of a saving interest in Jesus Christ: but with grief and humble shame I do acknowledge, I have fallen into sin often since that. Though I do not—dare not—allow of any one transgression, yet hitherto I have not been (nor do I expect that while I am in this present world I ever shall be) able to live one day per-fectly free from all defects and sin. And since the Scriptures declare that there is not a just man upon earth (no, not among those of the highest attainments in grace) that doeth good and sinneth not [Eccl. 7:20], we are sure that this will be the case of all the children of God.

The universal experience and acknowledgement of this among the godly in every age is abundantly sufficient to confute the error of those who hold in an absolute sense that after a man is born again he cannot commit sin; especially, since the Holy Spirit condemns the persons who say they have no sin as deceiving themselves, as being destitute of the truth, and as making God a liar (1 John 1:8, 10). I have been also in heaviness through manifold temptations, and expect to be often so before I die. Thus were the Apostles and primitive Christians themselves. Thus was Luther, that man of God, who, as far as I can find, did not peremptorily, at least, hold election; and the great John Arndt was in the utmost perplexity, but a quarter of an hour before he died, and yet he was no predestinarian.

And if I must speak freely, I believe your fighting so strenuously against the doctrine of election and pleading so vehemently for a sinless perfection are among the reasons or culpable causes, why you are kept out of the liberties of the gospel, and from that full assurance of faith which they enjoy, who have experimentally tasted, and daily feed upon God's electing, everlasting love.

But perhaps you may say, that Luther and Arndt were no Christians, at least very weak ones. I know you think meanly of Abraham, though he was eminently called the friend of God: and, I believe, also of David, the man after God's own heart. No wonder, therefore, that in a letter you sent me not long since, you should tell me that no Baptist or Presbyterian writer whom you have read knew anything of the liberties of Christ. What? Neither Bunyan, Henry, Flavel, Halyburton, nor any of the New England and Scots divines? See, dear Sir, what narrow-spiritedness and want of charity arise from your principles, and then do not cry out against election any more on account of its being "destructive of meekness and love."

Fourth, I shall now proceed to another head. Says the dear Mr. Wesley, "How uncomfortable a thought is this, that thousands and millions of men, without any preceding offence or fault of theirs, were unchangeably doomed to everlasting burnings?"

But who ever asserted, that thousands and millions of men, *without any preceding offence or fault of theirs*, were unchangeably doomed to everlasting burnings? Do not they who believe God's dooming men to everlasting burnings, also believe, that God looked upon them as men fallen in Adam? And that the decree which ordained the punishment first regarded the crime by which it was deserved? How then are they doomed without any preceding fault? Surely Mr. Wesley will own God's justice in imputing Adam's sin to his posterity. And also, after Adam fell, and his posterity in him, God might justly have passed them *all* by, without sending his own Son to be a saviour for any one. Unless you heartily agree to both these points, you do not believe original sin aright. If you do own them, then you must acknowledge the doctrine of election and reprobation to be highly just and reasonable. For if God might justly impute Adam's sin to all, and afterwards have passed by all, then he might justly pass by *some*. Turn on the right hand, or on the left; you are reduced to an inextricable dilemma. And, if you would be consistent, you must either give up the doctrine of the imputation of Adam's sin, or receive the amiable doctrine of election, with a holy and righteous reprobation as its consequent. For whether you can believe it or not, the Word of God abides faithful: "The election hath obtained it, and the rest were blinded" [Rom. 11:7].

Your 17th paragraph, page 16, I pass over. What has been said on the 9th and 10th paragraphs, with a little alteration, will answer it. I shall only say, it is the doctrine of election that most presses me to abound in good works. I am willing to suffer all things for the elect's sake. This makes me to preach with comfort, because I know salvation does not depend on man's free will, but the Lord makes willing in the day of his power, and can make use of me to bring some of his elect home, when and where he pleases.

But, fifth, you say, "This doctrine has a direct manifest tendency to overthrow the whole Christian religion. For," say you, "supposing that eternal, unchangeable decree, one part of mankind must be saved, though the Christian revelation were not in being."

But, dear Sir, how does that follow? Since it is only by the Christian revelation that we are acquainted with God's design of saving his church by the death of his Son. Yea, it is settled in the everlasting covenant that this salvation shall be applied to the elect through the knowledge and faith of him. As the prophet says in Isaiah 53:11, "*By his knowledge* shall my righteous servant justify many.*" How then has the doctrine of election a direct tendency to overthrow the whole Christian revelation? Who ever thought that God's declaration to Noah, that seed-time and harvest should never cease, could afford an argument for the neglect of plowing or sowing? Or that the unchangeable purpose of God, that harvest should not fail, rendered the heat of the sun, or the influence of the heavenly bodies unnecessary to produce it? No more does God's absolute purpose of saving his chosen preclude the necessity of the gospel revelation, or the use of any of the means through which he has determined the decree shall take effect. Nor will the right understanding, or the reverent belief of God's decree, ever allow or suffer a Christian in any case to separate the means from the end, or the end from the means.

And since we are taught by the revelation itself that this was intended and given by God as a means of bringing home his elect, we therefore receive it with joy, prize it highly, use it in faith, and endeavour to spread it through all the world, in the full assurance, that wherever God sends it, sooner or later, it shall be savingly useful to all the elect within its call.

How then, in holding this doctrine, do we join with modern unbelievers in making the Christian revelation unnecessary? No, dear Sir, you mistake. Infidels of all kinds are on *your* side of the question. Deists, Arians, and Socinians arraign God's sovereignty and stand up for universal redemption. I pray God that dear Mr. Wesley's sermon, as it has grieved the hearts of many of God's children, may not also strengthen the hands of many of his most avowed enemies!

Here I could almost lie down and weep. "Tell it not in Gath, publish it not in the streets of Askelon; lest the daughters of the Philistines rejoice, lest the daughters of the uncircumcised triumph" [2 Sam. 1:20].

Further, you say, "This doctrine makes revelation contradict itself." For instance, say you, "The assertors of this doctrine interpret that text of Scripture, Jacob have I loved, but Esau have I hated, as implying that God, in a literal sense, hated Esau and all the reprobates from eternity!" And, when considered as fallen in Adam, were they not objects of his hatred? And might not God, of his own good pleasure, love or show mercy to Jacob and the elect—and yet at the same time do the reprobate no wrong? But you say, "God is love." And cannot God be love, unless he shows the same mercy to all?

Again, says dear Mr. Wesley, "They infer from that text, 'I will have mercy on whom I will have mercy,' that God is merciful only to some men, viz. the elect; and that he has mercy for those only, flatly contrary to which is the whole tenor of the Scripture, as is that express declaration in particular, 'The Lord is loving to every man, and his mercy is over all his works.' "

And so it is, but not his *saving* mercy. God is loving to every man: he sends his rain upon the evil and upon the good. But you say, "God is no respecter of persons" [Acts 10:34]. No! For every one, whether Jew or Gentile, that believeth on Jesus, and worketh righteousness, is accepted of him. "But he that believeth not shall be damned"

[Mk. 16:16]. For God is no respecter of persons, upon the account of any outward condition or circumstance in life whatever; nor does the doctrine of election in the least suppose him to be so. But as the sovereign Lord of all, who is debtor to none, he has a right to do what he will with his own, and to dispense his favours to what objects he sees fit, merely at his pleasure. And his supreme right herein is clearly and strongly asserted in those passages of Scripture, where he says, "Moses, I will have mercy on whom I will have mercy, and I will have compassion on whom I will have compassion" (Rom. 9:15; Exod. 33:19).

Further, from the text, "the children being not yet born, neither having done any good or evil, that the purpose of God according to election might stand, not of works, but of him that calleth; it was said unto her (Rebekah), The elder shall serve the younger" [Rom. 9:11–12]—you represent us as inferring that our predestination to life in no way depends on the foreknowledge of God.

But who infers this, dear Sir? For if foreknowledge signifies approbation, as it does in several parts of Scripture, then we confess that predestination and election *do* depend on God's foreknowledge. But if by God's foreknowledge you understand God's fore-seeing some good works done by his creatures as the foundation or reason of choosing them and therefore electing them, then we say that in this sense predestination does not any way depend on God's foreknowledge.

But I referred you, at the beginning of this letter, to Dr. Edwards's *Veritas Redux*, which I recommended to you also in a late letter, with Elisha Coles on *God's Sovereignty*. Be pleased to read these, and also the excellent sermons of Mr. Cooper of Boston in New England (which I also sent you) and I doubt not but you will see all your objections answered. Though I would observe, that after all our reading on both sides [of] the question, we shall never in this life be able to search out God's decrees to perfection. No, we must humbly adore what we cannot comprehend, and with the great Apostle at the end of our enquiries cry out, "O the depth [of the riches both of the wisdom and knowledge of God! how unsearchable are his judgments, and his ways past finding out! For who hath known the mind of the Lord? or who hath been his counsellor?" (Rom. 11:33–34)]—or with our Lord, when he was admiring God's sovereignty, "Even so, Father: for so it seemed good in thy sight" [Matt. 11:26].

However, it may not be amiss to take notice, that if those texts, "The Lord is . . . not willing that any should perish, but that all should come to repentance" [2 Pet. 3:9] and "I have no pleasure in the death of the wicked; but that the wicked turn from his way and live" [Ezek. 33:11]—and such like—be taken in their strictest sense, then no one will be damned.

But here's the distinction. God taketh no pleasure in the death of sinners, so as to delight simply in their death; but he delights to magnify his justice, by inflicting the punishment which their iniquities have deserved. As a righteous judge who takes no pleasure in condemning a criminal, may yet justly command him to be executed, that law and justice may be satisfied, even though it be in his power to procure him a reprieve.

I would hint further, that you unjustly charge the doctrine of *reprobation* with blasphemy, whereas the doctrine of *universal redemption*, as you set it forth, is really the highest reproach upon the dignity of the Son of God, and the merit of his blood. Consider whether it be not rather blasphemy to say as you do, "Christ not only died for those that are saved, but also for those that perish."

The text you have misapplied to gloss over this, see explained by Ridgely, Edwards, Henry; and I purposely omit answering your texts myself so that you may be brought to read such treatises, which, under God, would show you your error. You cannot make good the assertion that Christ died for them that perish without holding (as Peter Bohler, one of the Moravian brethren, in order to make out universal redemption, lately frankly confessed in a letter) that all the damned souls would hereafter be brought out of hell. I cannot think Mr. Wesley is thus minded. And yet unless this can be proved, universal redemption, taken in a literal sense, falls entirely to the ground. For how can all be universally redeemed, if all are not finally saved?

Dear Sir, for Jesus Christ's sake, consider how you dishonour God by denying election. You plainly make salvation depend not on *God's free grace*, but on *man's free will*; and if thus, it is more than probable, Jesus Christ would not have had the satisfaction of seeing the fruit of his death in the eternal salvation of one soul. Our preaching would then be vain, and all invitations for people to believe in him would also be in vain.

But, blessed be God, our Lord knew for whom he died. There was an eternal compact between the Father and the Son. A certain number was then given him as the purchase and reward of his obedience and death. For these he prayed (Jn. 17:9), and *not for the world*. For these elect ones, and these only, he is now interceding, and with their salvation he will be fully satisfied.

I purposely omit making any further particular remarks on the several last pages of your sermon. Indeed had not your name, dear Sir, been prefixed to the sermon, I could not have been so uncharitable as to think you were the author of such sophistry. You beg the question, in saying that God has declared, (notwithstanding you own, I suppose, some will be damned) that he will save all—*i.e.*, every individual person. You take it for granted (for solid proof you have none) that God is unjust, if he passes by any, and then you exclaim against the "*horrible decree*": and yet, as I before hinted, in holding the doctrine of original sin, you profess to believe that he might justly have passed by all.

Dear, dear Sir, O be not offended! For Christ's sake be not rash! Give yourself to reading. Study the covenant of grace. Down with your carnal reasoning. Be a little child; and then, instead of pawning your salvation, as you have done in a late hymn book, if the doctrine of *universal redemption* be not true; instead of talking of *sinless perfection*, as you have done in the preface to that hymn book, and making man's salvation to depend on his *own free will*, as you have in this sermon; you will compose a hymn in praise of sovereign distinguishing love. You will caution believers against striving to work a perfection out of their own hearts, and print another sermon the reverse of this, and entitle it "Free Grace *Indeed*." Free, not because free to all; but free, because God may withhold or give it to whom and when he pleases.

Till you do this, I must doubt whether or not you know yourself. In the meanwhile, I cannot but blame you for censuring the clergy of our church for not keeping to their articles, when you yourself by your principles, positively deny the 9th, 10th and 17th.

Dear Sir, these things ought not so to be. God knows my heart, as I told you before, so I declare again, nothing but a single regard to the honour of Christ has forced this letter from me. I love and honour you for his sake; and when I come to judgment, will thank you before men and angels, for what you have, under God, done for my soul.

There, I am persuaded, I shall see dear Mr. Wesley convinced of election and everlasting love. And it often fills me with pleasure to think how I shall behold you casting your crown down at the feet of the Lamb, and as it were filled with a holy blushing for opposing the divine sovereignty in the manner you have done.

But I hope the Lord will show you this before you go hence. O how do I long for that day! If the Lord should be pleased to make use of this letter for that purpose, it would abundantly rejoice the heart of, dear and honoured Sir,

Your affectionate, though unworthy brother and servant in Christ,

GEORGE WHITEFIELD

One of Whitefield's early sermons, "The Almost Christian" explores what it truly means to be a Christian. Whitefield pulls no punches: to be an almost Christian is to be totally lost. This sermon gives the reader a look at Whitefield's passion as an evangelist. His heart's desire is to see as many people come to know Christ as he possibly can. As this was a common theme in the eighteenth-century revivals, John Wesley preached a sermon with the same title.

SERMON 43: "THE ALMOST CHRISTIAN"

"Almost thou persuadest me to be a Christian." (Acts 26:28)

The chapter, out of which the text is taken, contains an admirable account which the great St. Paul gave of his wonderful conversion from Judaism to Christianity, when he was called to make his defense before Festus a Gentile governor, and king Agrippa. Our blessed Lord had long since foretold, that when the Son of man should be lifted up, "his disciples should be brought before kings and rulers, for his name's sake, for a testimony unto them" [see Matt. 10:18]. And very good was the design of infinite wisdom in thus ordaining it; for Christianity being, from the beginning, a doctrine of the Cross, the princes and rulers of the earth thought themselves too high to be instructed by such mean teachers, or too happy to be disturbed by such unwelcome truths; and therefore would have always continued strangers to Jesus Christ, and him crucified, had not the apostles, by being arraigned before them, gained opportunities of preaching to them "Jesus and the resurrection" [Acts 17:8]. St. Paul knew full well that this was the main reason, why his blessed Master permitted his enemies at this time to arraign him at a public bar; and therefore, in compliance with the divine will, thinks it not sufficient, barely to make his defense, but endeavors at the same time to convert his judges. And this he did with such demonstration of the spirit, and of power, that Festus, unwilling to be convinced by the strongest evidence, cries out with a loud voice, "Paul, much learning doth make thee mad" [Acts 26:24]. To which the brave apostle (like a true follower of the holy Jesus) meekly replies, ["]I am not mad, most noble Festus, but speak forth the words of truth and soberness" [v. 25]. But in all probability, seeing king Agrippa more affected with his discourse, and observing in him an inclination to know the truth, he applies himself more particularly to him. "The king knoweth of these things; before whom also I speak freely; for I am persuaded that none of these things are hidden from him" [v. 26]. And then, that if possible he might complete his wished-for conversion, he with an inimitable strain of oratory, addresses himself still more closely, "King Agrippa, believest thou the prophets? I know that thou believest them" [see v. 27]. At which the passions of the king began to work so strongly, that he was obliged in open court, to own himself affected by the prisoner's preaching, and ingenuously to cry out, "Paul, almost thou persuadest me to be a Christian" [v. 28].

Which words, taken with the context, afford us a lively representation of the different reception, which the doctrine of Christ's ministers, who come in the power and spirit of St. Paul, meets with now-a-days in the minds of men. For notwithstanding they, like this great apostle, "speak forth the words of truth and soberness;" and with such energy and power, that all their adversaries cannot justly gainsay or resist; yet, too many, with the noble Festus before-mentioned, being like him, either too proud to be taught, or too sensual, too careless, or too worldly-minded to live up to the doctrine, in order to excuse themselves, cry out, that "much learning, much study, or, what is more unaccountable, much piety, hath made them mad." And though, blessed be God! All do not thus disbelieve our report; yet amongst those who gladly receive the word, and confess that we speak the words of truth and soberness, there are so few, who arrive at any higher degree of piety than that of Agrippa, or are any farther persuaded than to be almost Christians, that I cannot but think it highly necessary to warn my dear hearers of the danger of such a state. And therefore, from the words of the text, shall endeavor to show these three things:

FIRST, What is meant by an almost-Christian.

SECONDLY, What are the chief reasons, why so many are no more than almost Christians.

THIRDLY, I shall consider the ineffectualness, danger, absurdity, and uneasiness which attends those who are but almost Christians; and then conclude with a general exhortation, to set all upon striving not only be almost, but altogether Christians.

7.1 All Whitefield needed to preach was his open Bible. He was not tied to a manuscript or notes.

I. And, FIRST, I am to consider what is meant by an almost Christian.

An almost Christian, if we consider him in respect to his duty to God, is one that halts between two opinions; that wavers between Christ and the world; that would reconcile God and Mammon, light and darkness, Christ and Belial. It is true, he has an inclination to religion, but then he is very cautious how he goes too far in it: his false heart is always crying out, Spare thyself, do thyself no harm. He prays indeed, that "God's will may be done on earth, as it is in heaven" [see Matt. 6:10]. But notwithstanding, he is very partial in his obedience, and fondly hopes that God will not be extreme to mark every thing that he willfully does amiss; though an inspired apostle has told him, that "he who offends in one point is guilty of all" [see James 2:10]. But chiefly, he is one that depends much on outward ordinances, and on that account looks upon himself as righteous, and despises others; though at the same time he is as great a stranger to the divine life as any other person whatsoever. In short, he is fond of the form, but never experiences the power of godliness in his heart. He goes on year after year, attending on the means of grace, but then, like Pharaoh's lean kine, he is never the better, but rather the worse for them.

If you consider him in respect to his neighbor, he is one that is strictly just to all; but then this does not proceed from any love to God or regard to man, but only through a principle of self-love: because he knows dishonesty will spoil his reputation, and consequently hinder his thriving in the world.

He is one that depends much upon being negatively good, and contents himself with the consciousness of having done no one any harm; though he reads in the gospel, that "the unprofitable servant was cast into outer darkness" [see Matt. 25:20], and the barren fig-tree was cursed and dried up from the roots, not for bearing bad, but no fruit.

He is no enemy to charitable contributions in public, if not too frequently recommended: but then he is unacquainted with the kind offices of visiting the sick and imprisoned, clothing the naked, and relieving the hungry in a private manner. He thinks that these things belong only to the clergy, though his own false heart tells him, that nothing but pride keeps him from exercising these acts of humility; and that Jesus Christ, in the 25th chapter of St. Matthew, condemns persons to everlasting punishment, not merely for being fornicators, drunkards, or extortioners, but for neglecting these charitable offices, "When the Son of man shall come in his glory, he shall set the sheep on his right-hand, and the goats on his left. And then shall he say unto them on his left hand, depart from me, ye cursed, into everlasting fire prepared for the devil and his angels: for I was an hungered, and ye gave me no meat; I was thirsty, and ye gave me no drink; I was a stranger, and ye took me not in; naked, and ye clothed me not; sick and in prison, and ye visited me not. Then shall they also say, Lord, when saw we thee an hungered, or a-thirst, or a stranger, or naked, or sick, or in prison, and did not minister unto thee? Then shall he answer them, Verily I say unto you, inasmuch as ye have not done it unto one of the least of these my brethren, ye did it not unto me: and these shall go away into everlasting punishment . . ." [see vv. 31, 33, 41–46]. I thought proper to give you this whole passage of scripture at large, because our Savior lays such a particular stress upon it; and yet it is so little regarded, that were we to judge by the practice of Christians, one should be tempted to think there were no such verses in the Bible.

But to proceed in the character of an ALMOST CHRISTIAN: If we consider him in respect of himself; as we said he was strictly honest to his neighbor, so he is likewise strictly sober in himself: but then both his honesty and sobriety proceed from the same principle of a false self-love. It is true, he runs not into the same excess of riot with other men; but then it is not out of obedience to the laws of God, but either because his constitution will not away with intemperance; or rather because he is cautious of forfeiting his reputation, or unfitting himself for temporal business. But though he is so prudent as to avoid intemperance and excess, for the reasons before-mentioned; yet he always goes to the extremity of what is lawful. It is true, he is no drunkard; but then he has no CHRISTIAN SELF-DENIAL. He cannot think our Savior to be so austere a Master, as to deny us to indulge ourselves in some particulars: and so by this means he is destitute of a sense of true religion, as much as if he lived in debauchery, or any other crime whatever. As to settling his principles as well as practice, he is guided more by the world, than by the word of God: for his part, he cannot think the way to heaven so narrow as some would make it; and therefore considers not so much what scripture requires, as what such and such a good man does, or what will best suit his own corrupt inclinations. Upon this account, he is not only very cautious himself, but likewise very careful of young converts, whose faces are set heavenward; and therefore is always acting the devil's part, and bidding them spare themselves, though they are doing no more than what the scripture strictly requires them to do: The consequence of which is, that "he suffers not himself to enter into the kingdom of God, and those that are entering in he hinders" [see Matt. 23:13].

Thus lives the almost Christian: not that I can say, I have fully described him to you; but from these outlines and sketches of his character, if your consciences have done their proper office, and made a particular application of what has been said to your own hearts, I cannot but fear that some of you may observe some features in his picture, odious as it is, to near resembling your own; and therefore I cannot but hope, that you will join with the apostle in the words immediately following the text, and wish yourselves "to be not only almost, but altogether Christians" [see Acts 26:29].

II. I proceed to the second general thing proposed; to consider the reasons why so many are no more than almost Christians.

1. And the first reason I shall mention is, because so many set out with false notions of religion; though they live in a Christian country, yet they know not what Christianity is. This perhaps may be esteemed a hard saying, but experience sadly evinces the truth of it; for some place religion in being

of this or that communion; more in morality; most in a round of duties, and a model of performances; and few, very few acknowledge it to be, what it really is, a thorough inward change of nature, a divine life, a vital participation of Jesus Christ, an union of the soul with God; which the apostle expresses by saying, "He that is joined to the Lord is one spirit" [see 1 Cor. 6:17]. Hence it happens, that so many, even of the most knowing professors, when you come to converse with them concerning the essence, the life, the soul of religion, I mean our new birth in Jesus Christ, confess themselves quite ignorant of the matter, and cry out with Nicodemus, "How can this thing be?" [see John 3:9]. And no wonder then, that so many are only almost Christians, when so many know not what Christianity is: no marvel, that so many take up with the form, when they are quite strangers to the power of godliness; or content themselves with the shadow, when they know so little about the substance of it. And this is one cause why so many are almost, and so few are altogether Christians.

2. A second reason that may be assigned why so many are no more than almost Christians, is a servile fear of man: multitudes there are and have been, who, though awakened to a sense of the divine life, and have tasted and felt the powers of the world to come; yet out of a base sinful fear of being counted singular, or contemned by men, have suffered all those good impressions to wear off. It is true, they have some esteem for Jesus Christ; but then, like Nicodemus, they would come to him only by night: they are willing to serve him; but then they would do it secretly, for fear of the Jews: they have a mind to see Jesus, but then they cannot come to him because of the press, and for fear of being laughed at, and ridiculed by those with whom they used to sit at meat. But well did our Savior prophesy of such persons, "How can ye love me, who receive honor one of another?" [see John 5:44]. Alas!

have they never read, that "the friendship of this world is enmity with God" [see James 4:4]; and that our Lord himself has threatened, "Whosoever shall be ashamed of me or of my words, in this wicked and adulterous generation, of him shall the Son of man be ashamed, when he cometh in the glory of his Father and of his holy angels" [see Mark 8:38]? No wonder that so many are no more than almost Christians, since so many "love the praise of men more than the honor which cometh of God" [see John 12:43].

3. A third reason why so many are no more than almost Christians, is a reigning love of money. This was the pitiable case of that forward young man in the gospel, who came running to our blessed Lord, and kneeling before him, inquired "what he must do to inherit eternal life;" to whom our blessed Master replied, "Thou knowest the commandments, Do not kill, Do not commit adultery, Do not steal." To which the young man replied, "All these have I kept from my youth." But when our Lord proceeded to tell him, "Yet lackest thou one thing; Go sell all that thou hast, and give to the poor; he was grieved at that saying, and went away sorrowful, for he had great possessions!" Poor youth! He had a good mind to be a Christian, and to inherit eternal life, but thought it too dear, if it could be purchased at no less an expense than of his estate! And thus many, both young and old, now-a-days, come running to worship our blessed Lord in public, and kneel before him in private, and inquire at his gospel, what they must do to inherit eternal life: but when they find they must renounce the self-enjoyment of riches, and forsake all in affection to follow him, they cry, "The Lord pardon us in this thing! We pray thee, have us excused."

But is heaven so small a trifle in men's esteem, as not to be worth a little gilded earth? Is eternal life so mean a purchase, as not to deserve the temporary renunciation of a few transitory riches? Surely it is. But however inconsistent such a behavior may be, this inordinate love of money is too evidently the common and fatal cause, why so many are no more than almost Christians.

4. Nor is the love of pleasure a less uncommon, or a less fatal cause why so many are no more than almost Christians. Thousands and ten thousands there are, who despise riches, and would willingly be true disciples of Jesus Christ, if parting with their money would make them so; but when they are told that our blessed Lord has said, "Whosoever will come after him must deny himself;" like the pitiable young man before-mentioned, "they go away sorrowful" for they have too great a love for sensual pleasures. They will perhaps send for the ministers of Christ, as Herod did for John, and hear them gladly: but touch them in their Herodias, tell them they must part with such or such a darling pleasure; and with wicked Ahab they cry out, "Hast thou found us, O our enemy?" [see 1 Kings 21:20]. Tell them of the necessity of mortification and self-denial, and it is as difficult for them to hear, as if you was to bid them "cut off a right-hand, or pluck out a right-eye" [see Matt. 5:29–30]. They cannot think our blessed Lord requires so much at their hands, though an inspired apostle has commanded us to "mortify our members which are upon earth" [see Col. 3:5]. And who himself, even after he had converted thousands, and was very near arrived to the end of his race, yet professed that it was his daily practice to "keep under his body, and bring it into subjection, lest after he had preached to others, he himself should be a cast-away" [see 1 Cor. 9:27]!

But some men would be wiser than this great apostle, and chalk out to us what they falsely imagine an easier way to happiness. They would flatter us, we may go to heaven without offering violence to our sensual appetites; and enter into the strait gate without striving against our carnal inclinations.

And this is another reason why so many are only almost, and not altogether Christians.

5. The fifth and last reason I shall assign why so many are only almost Christians, is a fickleness and instability of temper.

It has been, no doubt, a misfortune that many a minister and sincere Christian has met with, to weep and wail over numbers of promising converts, who seemingly began in the Spirit, but after a while fell away, and basely ended in the flesh; and this not for want of right notions in religion, nor out of a servile fear of man, nor from the love of money, or of sensual pleasure, but through an instability and fickleness of temper. They looked upon religion merely for novelty, as something which pleased them for a while; but after their curiosity was satisfied, they laid it aside again: like the young man that came to see Jesus with a linen cloth about his naked body, they have followed him for a season, but when temptations came to take hold on them, for want of a little more resolution, they have been stripped of all their good intentions, and fled away naked. They at first, like a tree planted by the water-side, grew up and flourished for a while; but having no root in themselves, no inward principle of holiness and piety, like Jonah's gourd, they were soon dried up and withered. Their good intentions are too like the violent motions of the animal spirits of a body newly beheaded, which, though impetuous, are not lasting. In short, they set out well in their journey to heaven, but finding the way either narrower or longer than they expected, through an unsteadiness of temper, they have made an eternal halt, and so "returned like the dog to his vomit, or like the sow that was washed to her wallowing in the m[i]re" [see 2 Peter 2:22]!

But I tremble to pronounce the fate of such unstable professors, who having put their hands to the plough, for want of a little more resolution, shamefully look back. How shall

I repeat to them that dreadful threatening, "If any man draw back, my soul shall have no pleasure in him" [Heb. 10:38]. And again, "It is impossible" (that is, exceeding difficult at least) "for those that have been once enlightened, and have tasted of the heavenly gift, and the powers of the world to come, if they should fall away, to be renewed again unto repentance" [see Heb. 6:4–6]. But notwithstanding the gospel is so severe against apostates, yet many that begun well, through a fickleness of temper, (O that none of us here present may ever be such) have been by this means of the number of those that turn back unto perdition. And this is the fifth, and the last reason I shall give, why so many are only almost, and not altogether Christians.

III. Proceed we now to the general thing proposed, namely, to consider the folly of being no more than an almost Christian.

1. And the FIRST proof I shall give of the folly of such a proceeding is, that it is ineffectual to salvation. It is true, such men are almost good; but almost to hit the mark, is really to miss it. God requires us "to love him with all our hearts, with all our souls, and with all our strength" [see Deut. 6:5]. He loves us too well to admit any rival; because, so far as our hearts are empty of God, so far must they be unhappy. The devil, indeed, like the false mother that came before Solomon, would have our hearts divided, as she would have had the child; but God, like the true mother, will have all or none. "My Son, give me thy heart" [Prov. 23:26], thy whole heart, is the general call to all: and if this be not done, we never can expect the divine mercy.

Persons may play the hypocrite; but God at the great day will strike them dead, (as he did Ananias and Sapphira by the mouth of his servant Peter) for pretending to offer him all their hearts, when they keep back from him the greatest part. They may perhaps impose upon their fellow-creatures for a while; but he that enabled [Ahijah] to cry out, "Come in[,] thou wife of Jeroboam" [1 Kings 14:6], when she came disguised to inquire about her sick son, will also discover them through their most artful dissimulations; and if their hearts are not wholly with him, appoint them their portion with hypocrites and unbelievers.

2. But, SECONDLY, What renders an half-way-piety more inexcusable is, that it is not only insufficient to our own salvation, but also very prejudicial to that of others.

An almost Christian is one of the most hurtful creatures in the world; he is a wolf in sheep's clothing: he is one of those false prophets, our blessed Lord bids us beware of in his sermon on the mount, who would persuade men, that the way to heaven is broader than it really is; and thereby, as it was observed before, "enter not into the kingdom of God themselves, and those that are entering in they hinder." These, these are the men that turn the world into a luke-warm Laodicean spirit; that hang out false lights, and so shipwreck unthinking benighted souls in their voyage to the haven of eternity. These are they who are greater enemies to the cross of Christ, than infidels themselves: for of an unbeliever every one will be aware; but an almost Christian, through his subtle hypocrisy, draws away many after him; and therefore must expect to receive the greater damnation.

3. But, THIRDLY, As it is most prejudicial to ourselves and hurtful to others, so it is the greatest instance of ingratitude we can express towards our Lord and Master Jesus Christ. For did he come down from heaven, and shed his precious blood, to purchase these hearts of ours, and shall we only give him half of them? O how can we say we love him, when our hearts are not wholly with him? How can we call him our Savior, when we will not endeavor sincerely to approve ourselves to him, and so let him see the travail of his soul, and be satisfied!

Had any of us purchased a slave at a most expensive rate, and who was before involved in the utmost miseries and torments, and so must have continued for ever, had we shut up our bowels of compassion from him; and was this slave afterwards to grow rebellious, or deny giving us but half his service; how, how should we exclaim against his base ingratitude! And yet this base ungrateful slave thou art, O man, who acknowledgest thyself to be redeemed from infinite unavoidable misery and punishment by the death of Jesus Christ, and yet wilt not give thyself wholly to him. But shall we deal with God our Maker in a manner we would not be dealt with by a man like ourselves? God forbid! No. Suffer me, therefore,

To add a word or two of exhortation to you, to excite you to be not only almost, but altogether Christians. O let us scorn all base and treacherous treatment of our King and Savior, of our God and Creator. Let us not take some pains all our lives to go to h[e]aven, and yet plunge ourselves into hell [at] last. Let us give to God our whole hearts, and no longer halt between two opinions: if the world be God, let us serve that; if pleasure be a God, let us serve that; but if the Lord he be God, let us, O let us serve him alone. Alas! why, why should we stand out any longer? Why should we be so in love with slavery, as not wholly to renounce the world, the flesh, and the devil, which, like so many spiritual chains, bind down our souls, and hinder them from flying up to God. Alas! what are we afraid of? Is not God able to reward our entire obedience? If he is, as the almost Christian's lame way of serving him, seems to grant, why then will we not serve him entirely? For the same reason we do so much, why do we not do more? Or do you think that being only half religious will make you happy, but that going farther, will render you miserable and uneasy? Alas! this, my brethren, is delusion all over: for what is it but this half piety, this wavering between God and the world, that makes so many, that are seemingly well disposed, such utter strangers to the comforts of religion? They choose just so much of religion as will disturb them in their lusts, and follow their lusts so far as to deprive themselves of the comforts of religion. Whereas on the contrary, would they sincerely leave all in affection, and give their hearts wholly to God, they would then (and they cannot till then) experience the unspeakable pleasure of having a mind at unity with itself, and enjoy such a peace of God, which even in this life passes all understanding, and which they were entire strangers to before. It is true, if we will devote ourselves entirely to God, we must meet with contempt; but then it is because contempt is necessary to heal our pride. We must renounce some sensual pleasures, but then it is because those unfit us for spiritual ones, which are infinitely better. We must renounce the love of the world; but then it is that we may be filled with the love of God: and when that has once enlarged our hearts, we shall, like Jacob when he served for his beloved Rachel, think nothing too difficult to undergo, no hardships too tedious to endure, because of the love we shall then have for our dear Redeemer. Thus easy, thus delightful will be the ways of God even in this life: but when once we throw off these bodies, and our souls are filled with all the fullness of God, O! what heart can conceive, what tongue can express, with what unspeakable joy and consolation shall we then look back on our past sincere and hearty services. Think you then, my dear hearers, we shall repent we had done too much; or rather think you not, we shall be ashamed that we did no more; and blush we were so backward to give up all to God; when he intended hereafter to give us himself?

Let me therefore, to conclude, exhort you, my brethren, to have always before you the unspeakable happiness of enjoying God. And think withal, that every degree of holiness you neglect, every act of piety you omit, is a jewel taken out of your crown, a degree of blessedness lost in the vision of God. O! do but always think and act thus, and you will no longer be laboring to compound matters between God and the world; but, on the contrary, be daily endeavoring to give up yourselves more and more unto him; you will be always watching, always praying, always aspiring after farther degrees of purity and love, and consequently always preparing yourselves for a fuller sight and enjoyment of that God, in whose presence there is fullness of joy, and at whose right-hand there are pleasures for ever more. Amen! Amen!

George Whitefield preached this sermon in Philadelphia in 1746 shortly after British armies defeated French and Scottish Roman Catholic armies poised to restore the Stuarts to the English throne. While one of his lesser known sermons, it is an important piece to the puzzle of understanding Whitefield. First, he paints himself as a loyal British subject, but hints at his love for his adopted home and his love of freedom and liberty. Before too long, those twin themes of freedom and liberty would resound throughout the colonies. Sadly, Whitefield would not live long enough to hear "freedom ring" for his American flock.

SERMON 6: "BRITAIN'S MERCIES, AND BRITAIN'S DUTIES"

"That they might observe his statutes, and keep his laws." (Ps. 105:45)

Men, brethren and fathers, and all ye to whom I am about to preach the kingdom of God, I suppose you need not be informed, that being indispensably obliged to be absent on your late thanksgiving-day, I could not shew my obedience to the Governor's proclamation, as my own inclination led me, or as might justly be expected from, and demanded of me. But as the occasion of that day's thanksgiving is yet, and I trust ever will be, fresh in our memory, I cannot think that a discourse on the subject can even now be altogether unseasonable. I take it for granted further, that you need not be informed, that among the various motives which are generally urged to enforce obedience to the divine commands, that of love is the most powerful and cogent. The terrors of the law may afright and awe, but love dissolves and melts the heart. The love of Christ, says the great Apostle of the gentiles, constraineth us. Nay, love is so absolutely necessary for those that name the name of Christ, that without it, their obedience cannot truly be [styled] evangelical, or be acceptable in the sight of God. "Although," says the same Apostle, "I bestow all my Goods to feed the Poor, and though I give my Body to be burnt, and have not Charity" (*i.e.* unless unfeigned love to God, and to mankind for his great name's sake, be the principle of such actions, howsoever it may benefit others), "it profiteth me nothing" [see 1 Cor. 13:3]. This is the constant language of the lively oracles of God. And, from them it is equally plain, that nothing has a greater tendency to beget and excite such an obediential love in us than a serious and frequent consideration of the manifold mercies we receive time after time from the hands of our heavenly Father. The royal Psalmist, who had the honour of being [styled] *the man after* God's *own heart*, had an abundant experience of this. Hence it is, that whilst he is musing on the divine goodness, the fire of divine love kindles in his soul; and, "out of the abundance of his heart, his mouth speaketh" [see Luke 6:45] such grateful and extatic language as this—"What shall I render unto the Lord for all His Mercies?" [see Ps. 116:12] "Bless the Lord, O my Soul, and all that is within me bless his holy Name" [Ps. 103:1]. And why? "Who forgiveth all thine Iniquities, who healeth all thy Diseases, who redeemeth thy Life from Destruction, who crowneth thee with loving Kindness and tender Mercies" [Ps. 103:3–4]. And when the same holy man of God had a mind to stir up the people of the Jews to set about a national reformation, as the most weighty and prevailing argument he could make use of for that purpose, he lays before them, as it were, in a draught, many national mercies, and distinguishing deliverances, which had been conferred upon, and wrought out for them, by the most high God. The psalm to which the words of our text belong, is a pregnant proof of this; it being a kind of epitome or compendium of the whole Jewish history: At least it contains an enumeration of many signal and extraordinary blessings the Israelites had received from God, and also the improvement they were in duty bound to make of them, viz. "to observe his statutes and keep his laws."

To run through all the particulars of the psalm, or draw a parallel (which might with great ease and justice be done) between God's dealings with us and the Israelites of old—to enumerate all the national mercies bestow'd upon, and remarkable deliverances wrought out for the kingdom of Great Britain, from the infant state of William the Conqueror, to her present manhood, and more than Augustan maturity, under the auspicious reign of our dread and rightful sovereign King George the Second; howsoever pleasing and profitable it might be at any other time, would, at this juncture, prove, if not an irksome, yet an unseasonable undertaking.

The occasion of the late solemnity, I mean the suppression of a most horrid and unnatural rebellion will afford more than sufficient matter for a discourse of this nature, and furnish us with abundant motives to love and obey that glorious *Jehovah,* "who giveth Salvation unto Kings, and delivers His People from the hurtful Sword" [see Ps. 144:10].

Need I make an apology before this auditory, if, in order to see the greatness of our late deliverance, I should remind you of the many unspeakable blessings which we have for a course of years enjoy'd, during the reign of his present majesty, and the gentle mild administration under which we live? Without justly incurring the censure of giving flattering titles, I believe all who have eyes to see, and ears to hear, and are but a little acquainted with our publick affairs, must acknowledge, that we have one of the best of kings. It is now above nineteen years since he began to reign over us. And yet, was he to be seated on a royal throne, and were all his subjects placed before him; was he to address them as Samuel once addressed the Israelites, "Behold here I am, Old and Greyheaded, witness against me before the Lord, whose Ox have I taken? Or whose Ass have I taken? Or whom have I defrauded? Whom have I oppressed?" [see 1 Sam. 12:1–3]. They must, if they would do him justice, make the same answer as was given to Samuel, "Thou hast not defrauded us, nor oppressed us" [v. 4]. What Tertullus, by way of flattery, said to Felix, may with the strictest justice be applied to our sovereign, "By thee we enjoy great quietness, and very worthy deeds have been done unto our nation by thy providence" [see Acts 24:2]. He has been indeed *pater patriæ*, a father to our country, and, tho' old and greyheaded, has jeoparded his precious life for us in the high places of the field. Nor has he less deserved that great and glorious title which the Lord promises kings should sustain in the latter days, I mean, "a nursing Father of the Church" [see Is. 49:23]. For not only the Church of England, as by law established, but Christians of every denomination whatsoever have enjoyed their religious, as well as civil liberties. As there has been no authorized oppression in the state, so there has been no publickly allowed persecution in the church. We breathe indeed in a free air; as free (if not freer) both as to temporals and spirituals, as any nation under heaven. Nor is the prospect likely to terminate in his majesty's death, which I pray God long to defer. Our princesses are disposed of to Protestant powers. And we have great reason to be assured that the present heir apparent, and his consort, are like minded with their royal father. And I cannot help thinking, that it is a peculiar blessing vouchsafed us by the King of Kings, that his present majesty has been continued so long among us. For now his immediate successor (though his present situation obliges him, as it were, to lie dormant) has great and glorious opportunities, which we have reason to think he daily improves, of observing and weighing the national affairs, considering the various steps and turns of government, and consequently of laying in a large fund of experience to make him a wise and great prince, if ever God should call him to sway the British sceptre. Happy art thou, O England! Happy art thou, O America, who on every side are thus highly favoured!

But, alas! How soon would this happy scene have shifted, and a melancholy gloomy prospect have succeeded in its room, had the rebels gained their point, and a popish abjured pretender been forced upon the British throne! For, supposing his birth not to be spurious (as we have great reason to think it really was), what could we expect from one, descended from a father, who, when duke of York, put all Scotland into confusion, and afterwards, when crowned king of England, for his arbitrary and tyrannical government both in church and state, was justly obliged to abdicate the throne, by the assertors of British liberty? Or, supposing the horrid plot, first hatched in hell, and afterwards nursed at Rome, had taken place; supposing, I say, the old pretender should have exchanged his cardinal's cap for a triple crown, and have transferred his pretended title (as it is reported he has done) to his eldest son, what was all this for, but that, by being advanced to the popedom, he might rule both son and subjects with less controul, and, by their united interest, keep the three kingdoms of England, Scotland and Ireland, in greater vassalage to the see of Rome? Ever since this unnatural rebellion broke out, I have looked upon the young pretender as the Phaeton of the present age. He is ambitiously and presumptuously aiming to seat himself in the throne of our rightful sovereign King George, which he is no more capable of maintaining than Phaeton was to guide the *chariot of the sun*; and had he succeeded in his attempt, like him, would only have set the world on fire. It is true, to do him justice, he has deserved well of the church of Rome, and, in all probability, will hereafter be canonized amongst the noble order of their fictitious saints. But, with what an iron rod we might expect to have been bruized, had his troops been victorious, may easily be imagin'd from those cruel orders, found in the pockets of some of his officers, "*Give no quarter to the elector's troops.*" Add to this, that there was great reason to suspect, that, upon the first news of the success of the rebels, a general massacre was intended. So that if the Lord had not been on our side, Great Britain, not to say America, would, in a few weeks, or months, have been an Aceldama, a field of blood. Besides, was a popish pretender to rule over us, instead of being represented by a free parliament, and governed by laws made by their consent, as we now are, we should shortly have had only the shadow of one, and, it may be, no parliament at all. This is the native product of a popish government, and what the unhappy family, from which this young adventurer pretends to be descended, has always aimed at. Arbitrary principles he has sucked in with his mother's milk; and if he had been so honest, instead of that immature motto upon his standard, *Tandem triumphans*, only to have put, *Stet pro ratione voluntas*, he had given us a short, but true, portraiture of the nature of his intended, but, blessed be God, now defeated reign. And, why should I mention, that the loss of the national debt, and the dissolution of the present happy union between the two kingdoms, would have been the immediate consequences of his success, as he himself declares in his second manifesto, dated from Holyrood House? These are evils, and great ones too; but then they are only evils of a temporary nature. They chiefly concern the body, and must necessarily terminate in the grave. But, alas! what an inundation of spiritual mischiefs would soon have overflowed the church, and what unspeakable danger should we and our posterity have been reduced to in respect to our better parts, our precious and immortal souls? How soon would whole swarms of monks, Dominicans and friars, like so many locusts, have overspread and plagued the nation? With what winged speed would foreign titular bishops have posted over in order to take possession of their respective sees? How quickly would our universities have been filled with youths who have been sent abroad by their popish parents, in order to drink in all the superstitions of the church of Rome? What a speedy period would have been put to societies of all kinds, for *promoting Christian knowledge, and propagating the gospel in foreign parts*? How soon would our pulpits have every where been filled with those old antichristian doctrines, freewill, meriting by works, transubstantiation, purgatory, works of supererogation, passive obedience, non-resistance, and all the other abominations of the Whore of Babylon? How soon would our Protestant charity schools in England, Scotland and Ireland, have been pulled down, our Bibles forcibly taken from us, and ignorance every where set up as the mother of devotion? How soon should we have been deprived of that invaluable blessing, liberty of conscience, and been obliged to commence (what they falsely call) catholics, or submit to all the tortures which a bigoted zeal, guided by the most cruel principles, could possibly invent? How soon would that mother of harlots have made herself once more drunk with the blood of the saints, and the whole tribe even of free-thinkers themselves, been brought to this dilemma, either to die martyrs for (tho' I never yet heard of one that did so), or, contrary to all their most avow'd principles, renounce their great Diana, unassisted, unenlightened reason? But I must have done, lest while I am speaking against Antichrist, I should unawares fall myself, and lead my hearers into an antichristian spirit. True and undefiled religion will regulate our zeal, and teach us to treat even the man of sin, with no harsher language than that which the angel gave his grand employer Satan, "The Lord rebuke thee" [Zech. 3:2].

Glory be to his great name, the Lord has rebuked him, and that too at a time when we had little reason to expect such a blessing at God's hands. My dear hearers, neither the present frame of my heart, nor the occasion of your late solemn meeting, lead me to give you a detail of our publick vices tho' alas! they are so many, so notorious, and withal of such a crimson-dye, that a gospel minister would not be altogether inexcusable, was he, even on such a joyful occasion, "to lift up his voice like a trumpet, to shew the British nation their transgression, and the people of America their sin" [paraphrased from Is. 58:1]. However, tho' I would not cast a dismal shade upon the pleasing picture the cause of our late rejoicings set before us; yet thus much may, and ought to be said, *viz.* that, as God has not dealt so bountifully with any people as with us, so no nation under heaven have dealt more ungratefully with him. We have been, like Capernaum, lifted up to heaven in priviledges, and, for the abuse of them, like her, have deserved to be thrust down into hell. How well soever it may be with us, in respect to our civil and ecclesiastic constitution, yet in regard to our morals, Isaiah's description of the Jewish polity is too too applicable, "The whole Head is sick, the whole Heart is faint, from the Crown of the Head to the Sole of our Feet, we are full of Wounds and Bruises, and putrifying Sores" [see Is. 1:5–6]. We have, Jeshurun-like, "waxed fat and kicked" [Deut. 32:15]. We have played the harlot against God, both in regard to principles and practice. "Our Gold is become dim, and our fine Gold changed" [see Lam. 4:1]. We have crucified the Son of God afresh, and put him to an open shame. Nay, Christ has been wounded in the house of his friends. And every thing long ago seemed to threaten an immediate storm. But, Oh the long-suffering and goodness of God to-us-ward! When all things seemed ripe for destruction, and matters were come to such a crisis, that God's praying people began to think, that tho' Noah, Daniel and Job were living, they would only deliver their own souls; yet then, *in the midst of judgment, the most High remembered mercy,* and when a popish enemy was breaking in upon us like a flood, the Lord himself graciously lifted up a standard.

This to me does not seem to be one of the most unfavourable circumstances, which have attended this mighty deliverance; nor do I think you will look upon it as altogether unworthy your observation. Had this cockatrice indeed been crushed in the egg, and the young pretender driven back upon his first arrival, it would undoubtedly have been a great blessing. But not so great as that for which you lately assembled to give God thanks. For then his majesty would not have had so good an opportunity of knowing his enemies, or trying his friends. The British subjects would, in a manner, have lost the fairest occasion that ever offered to express their loyalty and gratitude to their rightful sovereign. France would not have been so greatly humbled; nor such an effectual stop have been put, as we trust there now is, to any such further popish plot, to rob us of all that is near and dear to us. "Out of the Eater therefore hath come forth Meat, and out of the Strong hath come forth Sweetness" [see Judg. 14:14]. The pretender's eldest son is suffered not only to land in the north-west highlands in Scotland, but in a little while to become a great band. This for a time is not believed, but treated as a thing altogether incredible. The friends of the government in those parts, not for want of loyalty, but of sufficient authority to take up arms, could not resist him. He is permitted to pass on with his terrible banditti, and, like the comet that was lately seen (a presage it may be of this very thing) spreads his baleful influences all around him. He is likewise permitted to gain a short liv'd triumph by a victory over a body of our troops at Preston Pans, and to take a temporary possession of the metropolis of Scotland. Of this he makes his boast, and informs the publick (they are his own words) that "*Providence had hitherto favoured him with* wonderful success, *led him in the way to victory, and to the capital of the ancient kingdom, tho' he came without foreign aid.*" Nay he is further permitted to press into the very heart of England. But now the Almighty interposes, "Hitherto he was to go, and no further" [see Job 38:11]. Here were his malicious designs to be staid. His troops of a sudden are driven back. Away they post to the Highlands, and there they are suffered not only to increase, but also to collect themselves into a large body, that having, as it were, what Caligula once wish'd Rome had, *but one neck, they might be cut off with one blow.*

The time, nature, and instrument of this victory deserve our notice. It was on a general fast-day, when the clergy and good people of Scotland were lamenting the disloyalty of their perfidious countrymen, and like Moses lifting up their hands, that Amalek might not prevail. The victory was total and decisive. Little blood was spilt on the side of the royalists. And to crown all, Duke William, his majesty's youngest son, has the honour of first driving back, and then defeating the rebel army—a prince, who in his infancy and nonage, gave early proofs of an uncommon bravery, and nobleness of mind—a prince, whose courage has increased with his years; who returned wounded from the battle of Dettingen, behav'd with surprizing bravery at Fontenoy, and now, by a conduct and magnanimity becoming the high office he sustains, like his glorious predecessor the prince of Orange, has once more delivered three kingdoms from the dread of popish cruelty and arbitrary power. What renders it still more remarkable is this—the day on which his highness gained this victory was the day after his birth-day, when he was ent[e]ring on the twenty sixth year of his age; and when Sullivan, one of the pretender's privy council, like another Ahit[h]ophel, advised the rebels to give our soldiers battle, presuming they were surfeited and overcharged with their yesterday's rejoicings, and consequently unfit to make any great stand against them. But glory be to God, who catches the wise in their own craftiness! His counsel, like Ahit[h] ophel's, proves abortive. Both general and soldiers were prepared to meet them. God "taught their hands to war, and their fingers to fight" [see Ps. 144:1], and brought the duke, after a bloody and deserved slaughter of some thousands of the rebels, with most of his brave soldiers, victorious from the field.

Were we to take a distinct view of this notable transaction, and trace it in all the particular circumstances that have attended it, I believe we must with one heart and voice confess, that if it be a mercy for a state to be delivered from a worse than a Catiline's conspiracy; or a church to be rescued from a hotter than a Dioclesian persecution—if it be a mercy to be delivered from a religion that turns plow-shares into swords, and pruning-hooks into spears, and makes it meritorious to shed Protestant blood—if it be a mercy to have all our present invaluable priviledges, both in church and state, secured to us more than ever—if it be a mercy to have these great things done for us at a season when, for our crying sins both church and state justly deserved to be over-turned—and if it be a mercy to have all this brought about for us, under God, by one of the blood royal, a prince acting with an experience far above his years—if any or all of these are mercies, then have you lately commemorated one of the greatest mercies that ever the glorious God vouchsafed the British nation.

And shall we not rejoice and give thanks? Should we refuse, would not the stones cry out against us? Rejoice then we may and ought: But, Oh! let our rejoicing be in the *Lord*, and run in a religious channel. This we find has been the practice of God's people in all ages. When he was pleased, with a mighty hand and outstretched arm to lead the Israelites through the Red Sea as on dry ground, "Then sang Moses and the Children of Israel; and Miriam the Prophetess, the Sister of Aaron, took a Timbrel in her Hand, and all the Women went out after her. And Miriam answered them, Sing ye to the Lord; for he hath triumphed gloriously" [see Ex. 15:1, 20–21]. When God subdued Jabin the king of Canaan before the children of Israel, "Then sang Deborah and Barak on that Day, saying, Praise ye the Lord for the avenging of Israel" [see Judg. 5:1–2]. When the ark was brought back out of the hands of the Philistines, David, tho' a king, danced before it. And, to mention but one instance more, which may serve as a general directory to us on this and such like occasions; When the great head of the church had rescued his people from the general massacre intended to be executed upon them by a cruel and ambitious Haman,

> Mordecai sent Letters unto all the Jews that were in all the Provinces of the King Ahasuerus, both nigh and far, to establish among them that they should keep the Fourteenth Day of the Month Adar, and the Fifteenth Day of the same yearly, as the Days wherein the Jews rested from their Enemies, and the Month which was turned unto them from

Sorrow unto Joy, and from Mourning into a good Day: That they should make them Days of Feasting and Joy, and of sending Portions one to another, and Gifts to the Poor.

And why should not we go and do likewise?

And shall we forget, on such an occasion, to express our gratitude to, and make honourable mention of those worthies, who have signalized themselves, and been ready to sacrifice both lives and fortunes at this critical juncture? This would be to act the part of those ungrateful Israelites, who are branded in the book of God, for not shewing kindness "to the House of Jerubbaal, namely Gideon, according to all the Goodness which he shewed unto Israel" [see Judg. 8:35]. Even a Pharoah could prefer a deserving Joseph, Ahasuerus a Mordecai, and Nebuchadnezzar a Daniel, when made instruments of signal service to themselves and people. "My Heart," says Deborah, "is towards" (*i.e.* I have a particular veneration and regard for) "the Governors of Israel, that offered themselves willingly. And blessed," adds she, "above Women shall Jael the Wife of Heber the Kenite be: For she put her Hand to the Nail, and her right Hand to the Workman's Hammer, and with the Hammer she smote Sisera, she smote off his Head, when she had pierced and stricken through his Temples" [see Judg. 5:9, 24, 26]. And shall not we say, "Blessed above men, let his royal highness the duke of Cumberland be: For, thro' his instrumentality, the great and glorious Jehovah hath brought mighty things to pass"? Should not our hearts be towards the worthy archbishop of York, the royal hunters, and those other English heroes, who "offered themselves so willingly"? Let the names of Blakeney, Bland and Rea, and all those who waxed valiant in fight, on this important occasion, live for ever in the British annals. Let that worthy clergyman who endured five hundred lashes from the cruel enemy (every one of which the generous duke said, he felt himself) be never forgotten by the ministers of Christ in particular. And let the name of that great that incomparably brave soldier of the king, and good soldier of Jesus Christ, Colonel Gardiner (excuse me if I here vent a sigh—he was my intimate friend), let his name, I say, be had in everlasting remembrance. His majesty has led us an example of gratitude. Acting like himself, upon the first news of this brave man's death, he sent immediate orders that his family should be taken care of. The noble duke gave a commission immediately to his eldest son. And the sympathizing prince of Hesse paid a visit of condolance to his sorrowful elect and worthy lady. The British parliament have made a publick acknowledgment of the obligation the nation lies under to his royal highness. And surely the least we can do, is to make a publick and grateful mention of their names, to whom under God, we owe so much gratitude and thanks.

But, after all, is there not an infinitely greater debt of gratitude and praise due from us, on this occasion, to him that is higher than the highest, even the King of Kings and Lord of Lords, the blessed and only Potentate? Is it not his arm, his strong [and] mighty arm (what instruments soever may have been made use of) that hath brought us this salvation? And may I not therefore address you in the exulting language of the beginning of this psalm from which we have taken our text,

> O give Thanks unto the Lord; call upon his Name, make known his Deeds among the People. Sing unto him, sing Psalms unto him: Talk ye of all his wondrous Works. Glory ye in his holy Name. Remember this marvellous Work which he hath done. [see Ps. 105:1–3, 5]

But shall we put off our good and gracious benefactor with a mere lip service? God forbid. Your worthy governour has honoured God in his late excellent proclamation, and God will honour him. But shall our thanks terminate with the day? No, in no wise. Our text reminds us of a more noble sacrifice, and points out to us the great end the almighty Jehovah proposes in bestowing such signal favours upon a people, viz. "That they should observe his Statutes, and keep his Laws."

This is the return we are all taught to pray that we may make to the most high God, the father of mercies, in the daily office of our church, viz.

> That our Hearts may be unfeignedly thankful, and that we may shew forth his Praise, not only with our Lips, but in our Lives, by giving up our selves to his Service, and by walking before him in Holiness and Righteousness all our Days.

Oh that these words were the real language of all that use them! Oh that there was in us such a mind! How soon would our enemies then flee before us, and God, even our own God, yet give us more abundant blessings!

And, why should we not *observe God's Statutes and keep his Laws*? Dare any say that any of his commands are grievous? Is not *Christ's* yoke, to a renewed soul, as far as renewed, easy; and his burden comparatively light? May I not appeal to the most refined reasoner, whether the religion of Jesus *Christ* be not a social religion? Whether the moral law, as explained by the Lord Jesus in the gospel, has not a natural tendency to promote the present good and happiness of a whole commonwealth, supposing they were obedient to it, as well as the happiness of every individual? From whence come wars and fightings amongst us? From what fountain do all those evils which the present and past ages have groaned under, flow, but from a neglect of the laws and statutes of our great and all-wise lawgiver Jesus of Nazareth? Tell me, ye men of letters, whether Lycurgus or Solon, Pythagoras or Plato, Aristotle, Seneca, Cicero, or all the ancient lawgivers and heathen moralists, put them all together, ever published a system of ethicks, any way worthy to be compared with the glorious system laid down in that much despised book (to use Sir Richard Steele's expression), emphatically called the scriptures? Is not the divine image and super-scription written upon every precept of the gospel? Do they not shine with a native intrinsick lustre? And, tho' many things in them are above, yet, is there any thing contrary to the strictest laws of right reason? Is not Jesus *Christ*, in scripture, [styled] the Word, the Λόγος the Reason? And is not his service justly [styled] [Λογικὴ] Λατρεία a reasonable service? What if there be mysteries in his religion? Are they not without all controversy great and glorious? Are they not mysteries of godliness, and worthy that God who reveals them? Nay, is it not the greatest mystery that men who pretend to reason, and call them-selves philosophers, who search into the *arcana naturæ*, and consequently find a mystery in every blade of grass, should yet be so irrational as to decry all mysteries in religion? Where is the scribe? Where is the wise? Where is the disputer against the Christian revelation? Does not every thing without and within us conspire to prove its divine original? And would not self-interest, if there was no other motive, excite us to *observe God's Statutes, and keep his Laws*?

Besides, considered as a Protestant people, do we not lie under the greatest obligations of any nation under heaven, to pay a chearful, unanimous, universal, persevering obedi-ence to the divine commands?

The wonderful and surprizing manner of God's bringing about a reformation in the reign of King Henry the Eighth—

his carrying it on in the blessed reign of King Edward the Sixth—his delivering us out of the bloody hands of Queen Mary, and destroying the Spanish invincible Armada, under her immediate Protestant successor Queen Elizabeth—his discovery of the popish plot under King James—the glorious revolution by King William—and, to come nearer to our own times, his driving away *four thousand five hundred Spaniards*, from a weak (tho' important) frontier colony, when they had, in a manner, actually taken possession of it—his giving us Louisbourg, one of the strongest fortresses of our enemies, contrary to all human probability, but the other day, into our hands (which may encourage our hopes of success, supposing it carried on in a like spirit, in our intended Canada expedition)—These, I say, with the victory which you have lately been commemorating, are such national mercies, not to mention any more, as will render us utterly inexcusable, if they do not produce a national reformation, and incite us all, with one heart, *to observe God's Statutes, and keep his Laws.*

Need I remind you further, in order to excite in you a greater diligence to comply with the intent of the text, that tho' the storm, in a great measure is abated by his royal highness's late success, yet we dare not say, *it is altogether blown over?*

The clouds may again return after the rain; and the few surviving rebels (which I pray God avert) may yet be suffered to make head against us. We are still engaged in a bloody, and in all probability, a tedious war, with two of the most inveterate enemies to the interests of Great Britain. And, tho' I cannot help thinking, that their present intentions are so iniquitous, their conduct so perfidious, and their schemes so directly derogatory to the honour of the most high God, that he will certainly humble them in the end; yet, as all things, in this life, *happen alike to all*, they may for a time be dreadful instruments of scourging us. If not, God has other arrows in his quiver to smite us with, besides the French king, his Catholick majesty, or an abjured pretender. Not only the sword, but plague, pestilence and famine are under the divine command. Who knows but he may say to them all, *Pass through these lands?* A fatal murrain has lately swept away abundance of cattle at home and abroad. A like epidemical disease may have a commission to seize our persons as well as our beasts. Thus God dealt with the Egyptians. Who dare say, He will not deal in the same manner with us? Has he not already given some symptoms of it? What great numbers upon the Continent have been lately taken off by the bloody-flux, small-pox, and yellow-fever? Who can tell what further judgments are yet in store? However, this is certain, the rod is yet hanging over us; and, I believe it will be granted, on all sides, that if such various dispensations of mercy and judgment, do not "teach the inhabitants of any land to learn righteousness" [see Is. 26:9], they will only ripen them for a greater ruin. Give me leave therefore, to dismiss you at this time with that solemn awful warning and exhortation with which the prophet Samuel, on a publick occasion, took leave of the people of Israel, "Only fear the Lord and serve Him, in Truth, with all your Heart: For consider, how great Things He hath done for you. But if ye shall still do wickedly" (I will not say as he did, "you shall be consumed"; but), "ye know not but you may provoke Him to consume both you and your King" [see 1 Sam. 12:24–25]. Which God of his infinite mercy prevent, for the sake of Jesus *Christ: To whom with the Father and the Holy Ghost, three Persons but one God, be all Honour and Glory, now and for evermore.* Amen, Amen.

Finis

7.2 Whitefield died young, arguing that he would rather "wear out than rust out" in the cause of Christ.

With his health failing, Whitefield decided to make one final trip to America. While not knowing whether he would ever return to England, there are hints in the sermon that Whitefield suspected his home-going was near. Whitefield's love for his flock is evident in the poignant message of Christ's watchful care in life and in death.

SERMON 59: "THE GOOD SHEPHERD"

"My sheep hear my voice, and I know them, and they follow me: And I give unto them eternal life, and they shall never perish, neither shall any man pluck them out of my hand." (John 10:27–28)

It is a common, and I believe, generally speaking, my dear hearers, a true saying, that bad manners beget good laws.

Whether this will hold good in every particular, in respect to the affairs of this world, I am persuaded the observation is very pertinent in respect to the things of another: I mean bad manners, bad treatment, bad words, have been over-ruled by the sovereign grace of God, to produce, and to be the cause of, the best sermons that were ever delivered from the mouth of the God-man, Christ Jesus.

One would have imagined, that as he came clothed with divine efficience, as he came with divine credentials, as he [spoke] as never man spake, no one should have been able to have resisted the wisdom with which he spake; one would imagine, they should have been so struck with the demon-stration of the Spirit, that with one consent they should all own that he was "that prophet that was to be raised up like unto Moses" [see Deut. 18:15]. But you seldom find our Lord preaching a sermon, but something or other that he said was cavilled at; nay, their enmity frequently broke through all good manners. They often, therefore, interrupted him whilst he was preaching, which shows the enmity of their hearts long before God permitted it to be in their power to shed his innocent blood. If we look no further than this chapter, where he presents himself as a good shepherd, one that laid down his life for his sheep; we see the best return he had, was to be looked upon as possessed or distracted; for we are told, that there was a division therefore again among the Jews for these sayings, and many of them said, "He hath a devil, and is mad; why hear ye him?" [John 10:20]. If the master of the house was served so, pray what are the servants to expect? Others, a little more sober-minded, said, "These are not the words of him that hath a devil;" the devil never used to preach or act in this way; "Can a devil open the eyes of the blind?" [v. 21]. So he had some friends among these rabble. This did not discourage our Lord; he goes on in his work; and we shall never, never go on with the work of God, till, like our Master, we are willing to go through good and through evil report; and let the devil see we are not so complaisant as to stop one moment for his barking at us as we go along.

We are told, that our Lord was at Jerusalem at the feast of the dedication, and it was winter; the feast of dedication held, I think, seven or eight days, for the commemoration of the restoration of the temple and altar, after its profanation by Antiochus. Now this was certainly a mere human institution, and had no divine image, had no divine superscription upon it; and yet I do not find that our blessed Lord and Master preached against it; I do not find that he spent his time about this; his heart was too big with superior things; and I believe when we, like him, are filled with the Holy Ghost, we shall not entertain our audiences with disputes about rites and ceremonies, but shall treat upon the essentials of the gospel, and then rites and ceremonies will appear with more indifference. Our Lord does not say, that he would not go up to the feast, for, on the contrary, he did go there, not so much as to keep the feast, as to have an opportunity to spread the gospel-net; and that should be our method, not to follow disputing; and it is the glory of the Methodists, that we have been now forty years, and, I thank God, there has not been one single pamphlet written by any of our preachers, about the non-essentials of religion.

Our Lord always made the best of every opportunity; and we are told, "he walked in the temple in Solomon's porch" [see v. 23]. One would have thought the scribes and Pharisees would have put him in one of their stalls, and have complimented him with desiring him to preach: no, they let him walk in Solomon's porch. Some think he walked by himself, no body choosing to keep company with him. Methinks I see him walking and looking at the temple, and foreseeing within himself how soon it would be destroyed; he walked pensive, to see the dreadful calamities that would come upon the land, for not knowing the day of its visitation; and it was to let the world see he was not afraid to appear in public: he walked, as much as to say, Have any of you any thing to say to me? and he put himself in their way, that if they had any things to ask him, he was ready to resolve them; and to show them, that though they had treated him so ill, yet he was ready to preach salvation to them.

In the 24th verse we are told, "Then came the Jews round about him, and said unto him, How long dost thou make us doubt?" They came round about him when they saw him walking in Solomon's porch; now, say they, we will have him, now we will attack him. And now was fulfilled that passage in the Psalms, "they compassed me about like bees" [Psalm 118:12], to sting me, or rather like wasps. Now, say they, we will get him in the middle of us, and see what sort of a man he is; we will see whether we cannot conquer him; they came to him, and they say, "How long dost thou make us to doubt?" [John 10:24]. Now this seems a plausible question, "How long dost thou make us to doubt?" Pray how long, sir, do you intend to keep us in suspense? Some think the words will bear this interpretation; Pray, sir, how long do you intend thus to steal away our hearts? They would represent him to be a designing man, like Absalom, to get the people on his side, and then set up himself for the Messiah; thus carnal minds always interpret good men's actions. But the meaning seems to be this, they were doubting concerning Christ; doubting Christians may think it is God's fault that they doubt, but, God knows, it is all their own. "How long dost thou make us to doubt?" I wish you would speak a little plainer, sir, and not let us have any more of your parables. Pray let us know who you are, let us have it from your own mouth; "if thou be the Christ, tell us plainly" [v. 24]; and I do not doubt, but they put on a very sanctified face, and looked very demure; "if thou be the Christ, tell us plainly," intending to catch him: if he do not say he is the Christ, we will say he is ashamed of his own cause; if he tells us plainly that he is the Christ, then we will impeach him to the governor, we will go and tell the governor that this man says he is the Messiah; now we know of no Messiah, but what is to jostle Caesar out of his throne. The devil always wants to make it believed that God's people, who are the most loyal people in the world, are rebels to the government under which they live; "If thou be the Christ, tell us plainly." Our Lord does not let them wait long for an answer; honesty can soon speak: "I told you, and ye believed not; the works that I do in my Father's name, they bear witness of me" [v. 25]. Had our Lord said, I am the Messiah, they would have taken him up; he knew that, and therefore he joined "the wisdom of the serpent" with "the innocence of the dove" [see Matt. 10:16]; says he, I appeal to my works and doctrine, and if you will not infer from them that I am the Messiah, I have no further argument. "But," he adds, "ye believe not, because ye are not of my sheep" [John 10:26]. He complains twice; for their unbelief was the greatest grief of heart to Christ: then he goes on in the words of our text, "My sheep hear my voice, and I know them, and they follow me. And I give unto them eternal life, and they shall never perish, neither shall any pluck them out of my hand" [vv. 27–28]. My sheep hear my voice; you think to puzzle me, you think to chagrin me with this kind of conduct, but you are mistaken; you do not believe on me, because you are not of my sheep. The great Mr. Stoddard of New England, (and no place under heaven produces greater divines than New England), preached once from these words, "But ye believe not, because ye are not of my sheep;" a very strange text to preach upon, to convince a congregation! Yet God so blessed it, that two [or] three hundred souls were awakened by that sermon: God grant such success to attend the labors of all his faithful ministers.

"My sheep hear my voice, and they follow me." It is very remarkable, there are but two sorts of people mentioned in scripture: it does not say that the Baptists and Independents, nor the Methodists and Presbyterians; no, Jesus Christ divides the whole world into but two classes, sheep and goats: the Lord give us to see this morning to which of these classes we belong.

But it is observable, believers are always compared to something that is good and profitable, and unbelievers are always described by something that is bad, and good for little or nothing.

If you ask me why Christ's people are called sheep, as God shall enable me, I will give you a short, and I hope it will be to you an answer of peace. Sheep, you know, generally love to be together; we say a flock of sheep, we do not say a herd of sheep; sheep are little creatures, and Christ's people may be called sheep, because they are little in the eyes of the world, and they are yet less in their own eyes. O, some people think, if the great men were on our side, if we had king[s], lords, and commons on our side, I mean if they were all true believers, O if we had all the kings upon the earth on our side! Suppose you had: alas! alas! do you think the church would go on the better? Why, if it were fashionable to be a Methodist at court, if it were fashionable to be a Methodist abroad, they would go with a Bible or a hymn-book, instead of a novel; but religion never thrives under too much sun-shine. "Not many mighty, not many noble, are called, but God hath chosen the foolish things of the world to confound the wise, and God hath chosen the weak things of the world to confound the things which are mighty" [1 Cor. 1:26–27]. Dr. Watts says,

Here and there I see a king, and here and there a great man, in heaven, but their number is but small.

Sheep are looked upon to be the most harmless, quiet creatures that God hath made: O may God, of his infinite mercy, give us to know that we are his sheep, by our having this blessed temper infused into our hearts by the Holy Ghost. "Learn of me," saith our blessed Lord; what to do? To work miracles? No; "Learn of me, for I am meek and lowly in heart" [Matt. 11:29]. A very good man, now living, said once, if there be any particular temper I desire more than another, it is the grace of MEEKNESS, quietly to bear bad treatment, to forget and to forgive: and at the same time that I am sensible I am injured, not to be overcome of evil, but to have grace given me to overcome evil with good. To the honor of Moses, it is declared, that he was the meekest man upon earth. Meekness is necessary for people in power; a man that is passionate is dangerous. Every governor should have a warm temper, but a man of an unrelenting, unforgiving temper, is no more fit for government than Phaethon to drive the chariot of the sun; he only sets the world on fire.

You all know, that sheep of all creatures in the world are the most apt to stray and be lost; Christ's people may justly, in that respect, be compared to sheep; therefore, in the introduction to our morning service, we say, "We have erred and strayed from thy ways like lost sheep." Turn out a horse, or a dog, and they will find their way home, but a sheep wanders about; he bleats here and there, as much as to [say], ["]Dear stranger, show me my way home again["]; thus Christ's sheep are too apt to wander from the fold; having their eye off the great Shepherd, they go into this field and that field, over this hedge and that, and often return home with the loss of their wool.

But at the same time sheep are the most useful creatures in the world; they manure the land, and thereby prepare it for the seed; they clothe our bodies with wool, and there is not the least part of a sheep but is useful to man: O my brethren, God grant that you and I may, in this respect, answer the character of sheep. The world says, because we preach faith we deny good works; this is the usual objection against the doctrine of imputed righteousness, but it is a slander, an impudent slander. It was a maxim in the first reformers' time, that though the ARMINIANS preached up good works, you must go to the CALVINISTS FOR THEM. Christ's sheep study to be useful, and to clothe all they can; we should labor with our hands, that we may have to give to all those that need.

Believers consider Christ's property in them; he says, "my sheep." O blessed be God for that little, dear, great word MY. We are his eternal election: "the sheep which thou hast given me" [see John 17:12], says Christ. They were given by God the Father to Christ Jesus, in the covenant made between the Father and the Son from all eternity. They that are not led to see this, I wish them better heads; though, I believe, numbers that are against it have got better hearts: the Lord help us to bear with one another where there is an honest heart.

He calls them "My sheep;" they are his by purchase. O sinner, sinner, you are come this morning to hear a poor creature take "his last farewell:" but I want you to forget the creature that is preaching, I want to lead you further than the Tabernacle: Where do you want to lead us? Why, to mount Calvary, there to see at what an expense of blood Christ purchased those whom he calls his own; he redeemed them with his own blood, so that they are not only his by eternal election, but also by actual redemption in time; and they were given to him by the Father, upon condition that he should redeem them by his heart's blood. It was a hard bargain, but Christ was willing to strike the bargain, that you and I might not be damned for ever.

They are his, because they are enabled in a day of God's power voluntarily to give themselves up unto him; Christ says of these sheep, especially, "that they hear his voice, and that they follow him." Will you be so good as to mind that! Here is an allusion to a shepherd; now in some places in scripture, the shepherd is represented as going after his sheep; 2 Sam 7:8, Ps 78:71. That is our way in England; but in the Eastern nations, the shepherds generally went before; they held up their crook, and they had a particular call that the sheep understood. Now, says Christ, "My sheep hear my voice." "This is my beloved Son," saith God, "hear ye him." And again, "The dead shall hear the voice of the Son of God, and live" [John 5:25]: now the question is, what do we understand by hearing Christ's voice?

First, we hear Moses' voice, we hear the voice of the law; there is no going to Mount Zion but by the way of mount Sinai; that is the right straight road. I know some say, they do not know when they were converted; those are, I believe, very few: generally, nay, I may say almost always, God deals otherwise. Some are, indeed, called sooner by the Lord than others, but before they are made to see the glory of God, they must hear the voice of the law; so you must hear the voice of the law before ever you will be savingly called unto God. You never throw off your cloak in a storm, but you hug it the closer; so the law makes a man hug close his corruptions, (Rom 7:7, 8, 9) but when the gospel of the Son of God shines into your souls, then they throw off the corruptions which they have hugged so closely; they hear his voice saying, Son, daughter, be of good cheer, thy sins, which are many, are all forgiven thee. "They hear his voice;" that bespeaks the habitual temper of their minds: the wicked hear the voice of the devil, the lusts of the flesh, the lusts of the eye, and the pride of life; and Christ's sheep themselves attended to it before conversion; but when called afterwards by God, they hear the voice of a Redeemer's blood speaking peace unto them, they hear the voice of his word and of his Spirit.

The consequence of hearing his voice, and the proof that we do hear his voice, will be to follow him. Jesus said unto his disciples, "If any man will come after me, let him deny himself, and take up his cross and follow me" [Matt. 16:24]. And it is said of the saints in glory, that "they followed the Lamb whithersoever he went" [see Rev. 14:4]. Wherever the shepherd turns his crook, and the sheep hear his voice, they follow him; they often tread upon one another, and hurt one another, they are in such haste in their way to heaven. Following Christ means following him through life, following him in every word and gesture, following him out of one clime into another. "Bid me come to thee upon the water" [see Matt. 14:28], said Peter: and if we are commanded to go over the water for Christ, God, of his infinite mercy, follow us! We must first be sure that the great Shepherd points his crook for us: but this is the character of a true servant of Christ, that he endeavors to follow Christ in thought, word, and work.

Now, my brethren, before we go further, as this is the last opportunity I shall have of speaking to you for some months, if we live; some of you, I suppose, do not choose, in general, to rise so soon as you have this morning; now I hope the world did not get into your hearts before you left your beds; now you are here, do let me entreat you to inquire whether you belong to Christ's sheep, or no. Man, woman, sinner, put thy hand to thy heart, and answer me. Didst thou ever hear Christ's voice so as to follow him, to give up thyself without reserve to him? I verily do believe from my inmost soul, (and that is my comfort, now I am about to take my leave of you,) that I am preaching to a vast body, a multitude of dear, precious souls, who, if it were proper for you to speak, would say, Thanks be unto God, that we can follow Jesus in the character of sheep, though we are ashamed to think how often we wander from him, and what little fruit we bring unto him; if that is the language of your hearts, I wish you joy; welcome, welcome, dear soul, to Christ. O blessed be God for his rich grace, his distinguishing, sovereign, electing love, by which he [has] distinguished you and me. And if he has been pleased to let you hear his voice, though the ministration of a poor miserable sinner, a poor, but happy pilgrim, may the Lord Jesus Christ have all the glory.

If you belong to Jesus Christ, he is speaking of you; for, says he, "I know my sheep." "I know them;" what does that mean? Why, he knows their number, he knows their names, he knows every one for whom he died; and if there were to be one missing for whom Christ died, God the Father would send him down again from heaven to fetch him. "Of all," saith he, "that thou hast given me, have I lost none." Christ knows his sheep; he not only knows their number, but the words speak the peculiar knowledge and notice he takes of them; he takes as much care of each of them, as if there were but that one single sheep in the world. To the hypocrite he saith, "Verily, I know you not" [see Matt. 25:12]; but he knows his saints, he is acquainted with all their sorrows, their trials, and temptations. He bottles up all their tears, he knows their domestic trials, he knows their inward corruptions, he knows all their wanderings, and he takes care to fetch them back again. I remember, I heard good Dr. Marryat, who was a good market-language preacher, once say at Pinner's hall, (I hope that pulpit will be always filled with such preachers), "God has got a great dog to fetch his sheep back," says he. Do not you know, that when the sheep wander, the shepherd sends his dog after them, to fetch them back again? So when Christ's sheep wander, he lets the devil go after them, and suffers him to bark at them, who, instead of driving them farther off, is made a means to bring them back again to Christ's fold.

There is a precious word I would have you take notice of, "I know them," that may comfort you under all your trials. We sometimes think that Christ does not hear our prayers, that he does not know us; we are ready to suspect that he has forgotten to be gracious; but what a mercy it is that he does know us. We accuse one another, we turn devils to one another, are accusers of the brethren; and what will support two of God's people when judged by one another but this, Lord, thou knowest my integrity, thou knowest how matters are with me?

But, my brethren, here is something better, here is good news for you; what is that? Say you: why, "I give unto them eternal life, and they shall never perish, neither shall any pluck them out of my hand." O that the words may come to your hearts with as much warmth and power as they did to mine thirty-five years ago. I never prayed against any corruption I had in my life, so much as I did against going into holy orders so soon as my friends were for having me go: and bishop Benson was pleased to honor me with peculiar friendship, so as to offer me preferment, or do any thing for me. My friends wanted me to mount the church betimes, they wanted me to knock my head against the pulpit too young; but how some young men stand up here and there and preach, I do not know how it may be to them; but God knows how deep a concern entering into the ministry and preaching, was to me; I have prayed a thousand times, till the sweat has dropped from my face like rain, that God, of his infinite mercy, would not let me enter the church before he called me to, and thrust me forth in, his work. I remember once in Gloucester (I know the room, I look up at the window when I am there and walk along the street; I know the window, the bedside, and the floor, upon which I have lain prostrate) I said, Lord, I cannot go, I shall be puffed up with pride, and fall into the condemnation of the devil; Lord, do not let me go yet; I pleaded to be at Oxford two or three years more; I intended to make an hundred and fifty sermons, and thought I would set up with a good stock in trade but I remember praying, wrestling, and striving with God; I said, I am undone, I am unfit to preach in thy great name, send me not, pray, Lord, send me not yet. I wrote to all my friends in town and country, to pray against the bishop's solicitations, but they insisted I should go into orders before I was twenty-two. After all the solicitations, these words came into my mind, "My sheep hear my voice, and none shall pluck them out of my hand." O may the words be blessed to you, my dear friends, that I am parting with, as they were to me when they came warm upon my heart; then, and not till then, I said, Lord, I will go, send me when thou wilt. I remember when I was in a place called Dover-Island, near Georgia, we put in with bad winds; I had an hundred and fifty in family to maintain, and not a single farthing to do it with, in the dearest part of the king's dominions; I remember, I told a minister of Christ, now in heaven, "I had these words once, sir, 'Nothing shall pluck you out of my hand.'" "O", says he, "take comfort from them, you may be sure God will be as good as his word, if he never tells you so again." And our Lord knew his poor sheep would be always doubting they should never reach heaven, therefore says he, "I give to them eternal life, and they shall never perish."

Here are in our text three blessed declarations, or promises:

First. I KNOW THEM.
Second. THEY SHALL NEVER PERISH; though they often think they shall perish by the hand of their lusts and

corruptions; they think they shall perish by the deceitfulness of their hearts; but Christ says, "They shall never perish." I have brought them out of the world to myself, and do you think I will let them go to hell after that? "I give to them eternal life;" pray mind that; not, I will, but I do. Some talk of being justified at the day of judgment; that is nonsense; if we are not justified here, we shall not be justified there. He gives them eternal life, that is, the earnest, the pledge, and assurance of it. The indwelling of the Spirit of God here, is the earnest of glory hereafter.

Third. NEITHER SHALL ANY PLUCK THEM OUT OF MY HAND. He holds them in his hand, that is, he holds them by his power; none shall pluck them thence. There is always something plucking at Christ's sheep; the devil, the lust of the flesh, the lust of the eye, and the pride of life, all try to pluck them out of Christ's hand. O my brethren, they need not pluck us, yet we help all three to pluck ourselves out of the hand of Jesus; but "none shall pluck them out of my hand," says Christ. "I give to them eternal life. I am going to heaven to prepare a place for them, and there they shall be." O my brethren, if it were not for keeping you too long, and too much exhausting my own spirits, I could call upon you to leap for you; there is not a more blessed text to support the final perseverance of the saints; and I am astonished any poor souls, and good people I hope too, can fight against the doctrine of the perseverance of the saints: What if a person say they should persevere in wickedness? Ah! That is an abuse of the doctrine; what, because some people spoil good food, are we never to eat it? But, my brethren, upon this text I can leave my cares, and all my friends, and all Christ's sheep, to the protection of Christ Jesus' never-failing love.

I thought this morning, when I came here, riding from the other end of the town, it was to me like coming to be executed publicly; and when the carriage turned just at the end of the walk, and I saw you running here, O, thinks I, it is like a person now coming just to the place where he is to be executed. When I went up to put on my gown, I thought it was just like dressing myself to be made a public spectacle to shed my blood for Christ. I take all heaven and earth to witness, and God and the holy angels to witness, that though I had preferment enough offered me, that though the bishop took me in his arms, and offered me two parishes before I was two-and-twenty, and always took me to his table; though I had preferment enough offered me when I was ordained, thou, O God, knowest, that when the bishop put his hand upon my head, I looked for no other preferment than publicly to suffer for the Lamb of God: in this spirit I came out, in this spirit I came up to this metropolis. I was thinking, when I read of Jacob's going over the brook with a staff, that I could not say I had so much as a staff, but I came up without a friend, I went to Oxford without a friend, I had not a servant, I had not a single person to introduce me; but God, by his Holy Spirit, was pleased to raise me up to preach for his great name's sake: through his divine Spirit I continue to this day, and feel my affections are as [strong] as ever towards the work and the people of the living God. The congregations at both ends of the town are dear to me: God has honored me to build this and the other place; and, blessed be his name, when he called me to Georgia at first, and I left all London affairs to God's care, when I had most of the churches in London open to me, and had twelve or fourteen constables to keep the doors, that people might not crowd too much; I had offers of hundreds then to settle in London, yet I gave it all up to turn pilgrim for God, to go into a foreign clime; and I hope with that same single intention I am going now.

Now I must come to the hardest part I have to act; I was afraid when I came out from home, that I could not bear the shock, but I hope the Lord Jesus Christ will help me to bear it, and help you to give me up to the blessed God, let him do with me what he will. This is the thirteenth time of my crossing the mighty waters; it is a little difficult at this time of life; and though my spirits are improved in some degree, yet weakness is the best of my strength: but I am clear as light in my call and God fills me with a peace that is unutterable, which a stranger intermeddles not with: into his hands I commend my spirit; and I beg that this may be the language of your hearts: Lord, keep him, let nothing pluck him out of thy hands. I expect many a trial while I am on board, Satan always meets me there; but that God who has kept me, I believe will keep me. I thank God, I have the honor of leaving every thing quite well and easy at both ends of the town; and, my dear hearers, my prayers to God shall be, that nothing may pluck you out of Christ's hands. Witness against me, if I ever set up a party for myself. Did ever any minister, or could any minister in the world say, that I ever spoke against any one going to any dear minister? I thank God, that he has enabled me to be always strengthening the hands of all, though some have afterwards been ashamed to own me. I declare to you, that I believe God will be with me, and will strengthen me; and I believe it is in answer to your prayers that God is pleased to revive my spirits: may the Lord help you to pray on. If I am drowned in the waves, I will say, while I am drowning, Lord, take care of my London, take care of my English friends, let nothing pluck them out of thy hands.

And as Christ has given us eternal life, O my brethren, some of you, I doubt not, will be gone to him before my return; but, my dear brethren, my dear hearers, never mind that; we shall part, but it will be to meet again for ever. I dare not meet you now, I cannot bear your coming to me, to part from me; it cuts me to the heart, and quite overcomes me, but by and by all parting will be over, and all tears shall be wiped away from our eyes. God grant that none that weep now at my parting, may weep at our meeting at the day of judgment; and if you never were among Christ's sheep before, may Christ Jesus bring you now. O come, come, see what it is to have eternal life; do not refuse it; haste, sinner, haste away: may the great, the good Shepherd, draw your souls. Oh! If you never heard his voice before, God grant you may hear it now; that I may have this comfort when I am gone, that I had the last time of my leaving you, that some souls are awakened at the parting sermon. O that it may be a farewell sermon to you; that it may be a means of your taking a farewell of the world, the lust of the flesh, the lust of the eye, and the pride of life. O come! Come! Come! To the Lord Jesus Christ; to him I leave you.

And you, dear sheep, that are already in his hands, O may God keep you from wandering; God keep you near Christ's feet; I do not care what shepherds keep you, so as you are kept near the great Shepherd and Bishop of souls. The Lord God keep you, lift up the light of his countenance upon you, and give you peace. Amen.

CONTINUING THE JOURNEY:
A BRIEF GUIDE TO WORKS BY
AND ABOUT GEORGE WHITEFIELD

George Whitefield was, first and foremost, a preacher. It is not surprising that the vast majority of his written works consist of either sermon manuscripts or transcriptions of sermons recorded by others. The good news for students of Whitefield is that these are readily available in print and in electronic formats. His sermons provide the perfect introduction to the work of the Grand Itinerant, as they read today as fresh and as powerful as they did when Whitefield preached them.

Works by Whitefield

There are several good anthologies of Whitefield's sermons available. *Select Sermons of George Whitefield*, published by Banner of Truth (1990), and A. R. Buckland's *Selected Sermons of George Whitefield* (1904) are helpful collections. John Gillies's *Memoirs of Rev. George Whitefield* (1838), while dated, contains more complete sermons of Whitefield than the two previous works combined. The Internet has allowed for Whitefield's sermons to have a much greater accessibility, with nearly sixty of his sermons available at sites such as http://www.ccel.org/ccel/whitefield/sermons.ii.html.

Other than sermons, Whitefield also left behind copies of his journals and letters. Sadly, Whitefield did not keep a journal regularly throughout his entire life. The journals that he kept regarding his early life and ministry are available in one volume published by Banner of Truth (1992). Banner of Truth also published a volume that includes a limited number of his letters written from 1734 to 1742 (1976).

Books about Whitefield

Whitefield's popularity led to a flurry of publishing about him both during his life and in the two and a half centuries since his death. Among the supporters and detractors, a number of volumes stand out as "must reads" for those wishing to further their study of George Whitefield.

One of the early biographies that kept Whitefield's memory alive for future generations has already been mentioned: John Gillies's *Memoirs of Rev. George Whitefield* (1838). While original copies may be difficult to find, reprints are readily available. The benefit of Gillies's work is its "chronological proximity" to Whitefield's time and its collection of Whitefield's sermons. Luke Tyerman's two-volume biography of Whitefield (1890) should be read together with his biography of John Wesley. Tyerman was more theologically compatible with John Wesley, so his biography of Whitefield is not nearly as complimentary as others might be. Yet even in his critique of Whitefield, he realizes the vital role he played in the revivals of the eighteenth century.

Whitefield biographies continued to roll off the presses through the twentieth and into the twenty-first centuries. The definitive biography of Whitefield is arguably that written by Arnold Dallimore (1979). His exhaustive research and lively writing style combine to draw readers into the life and work of Whitefield and to hold their attention through both lengthy volumes. More recently, E. A. Johnston, in his *George Whitefield: A Definitive Biography* (2009), has offered a two-volume biography of Whitefield in the spirit of Dallimore. While his is not nearly as well known or as accessible as Dallimore's work, Johnston had access to documents that were unavailable in Dallimore's day. This fact alone makes his work an important companion to earlier biographies.

More recent scholarship has focused on more specific aspects of Whitefield's life and ministry. This has allowed the authors to go deeper into the areas that a broader biography might only mention. Harry Stout's *The Divine Dramatist: George Whitefield and the Rise of Modern Evangelicalism* (1991) highlights Whitefield's genius in adapting his natural acting abilities to his pulpit ministry and his harnessing of fellow preachers and the press to spread news of the revivals. Frank Lambert suggests that Whitefield was "a pioneer in the commercialization of religion" and that he, along with Jonathan Edwards and others, helped to "invent" the Great Awakening. While his conclusions are certainly controversial, his *"Pedlar in Divinity": George Whitefield and the Transatlantic Revivals* offers a slightly different perspective on the beginnings, spread, and interconnectedness of the eighteenth-century revivals.

Whitefield fell deeply in love with North America in general and with the Georgia colony in particular. His deep love for the people of Georgia is evident in Edward J. Cashin's *Beloved Bethesda: A History of George Whitefield's Home for Boys, 1740–2000* (2001). Founded in 1740, Bethesda Academy continues today based on the same principles of love for God, sound academics, and hard work that Whitefield envisioned nearly three centuries ago. Whitefield's passion for North America and his fear of arbitrary power caused him to be something of a prophetic voice in the years leading up to the American Revolution. Jerome Dean Mahaffey outlines this in *The Accidental Revolutionary: George White-field and the Creation of America* (2011).

Whitefield lived in an age when large-group evangelism was an effective outreach strategy. People would come from miles around to hear him and would swell the population of any town in which he preached. While Whitefield-style evangelism is still attempted by some today, many people are "turned off" to it thanks to the way it has been abused over the years and to the many other distractions of contemporary society. But even if the age of large-group evangelism is past, that does not mean that nothing can be learned from the Grand Itinerant. His sermons are as fresh today as they were when first preached. His passion for God and for lost souls is something all Christians should desire. These reasons are more than sufficient to continue the "tour" of the life and thought of George Whitefield.

BIBLIOGRAPHY

Belcher, Joseph. *George Whitefield: A Biography, with Special Reference to His Labors in America.* New York: American Tract Society, 1857.

Buckland, A. R. *Selected Sermons of George Whitefield.* Philadelphia: Union Press, 1904.

Cashin, Edward J. *Beloved Bethesda: A History of George Whitefield's Home for Boys, 1740–2000.* Macon, GA: Mercer University Press, 2001.

Dallimore, Arnold A. *George Whitefield: The Life and Times of the Great Evangelist of the Eighteenth-Century Revival,* 2 vols. Westchester, IL: Cornerstone Books, 1980.

Franklin, Benjamin. *The Life and Letters of Benjamin Franklin.* Eau Claire, WI: E. M. Hale, n.d.

Gaustad, Edwin Scott. *The Great Awakening in New England.* Gloucester, MA: Peter Smith, 1965.

Gillies, John. *Memoirs of Rev. George Whitefield.* Middletown, CT: Hunt & Noyes, 1838.

Henry, Stuart C. *George Whitefield: Wayfaring Witness.* New York: Abingdon, 1957.

Johnston, E. A. *George Whitefield: A Definitive Biography.* Cleveland: The Old Paths Publications, 2014.

Knight, Helen C. *Lady Huntington and Her Friends; or, The Revival of the Work of God in the Days of Wesley, Whitefield, Romaine, Venn, and Others in the Last Century.* New York: American Tract Society, 1853.

Lambert, Frank. *Inventing the "Great Awakening."* Princeton: Princeton University Press, 1999.

———. *"Pedlar in Divinity": George Whitefield and the Transatlantic Revivals.* Princeton: Princeton University Press, 1994.

MacFarlan, D. *The Revivals of the Eighteenth Century, Particularly at Cambuslang, with Three Sermons by the Rev. George Whitefield.* London: John Johnstone, 1988.

Mahaffey, Jerome Dean. *The Accidental Revolutionary: George Whitefield and the Creation of America.* Waco, TX: Baylor University Press, 2011.

Myers, Richmond E. *Sketches of Early Bethlehem.* Bethlehem, PA: Moravian College Alumni Association, 1981.

Noll, Mark A. *A History of Christianity in the United States and Canada.* Grand Rapids: Eerdmans, 1992.

Schwenk, James L. *Catholic Spirit: Wesley, Whitefield, and the Quest for Evangelical Unity in Eighteenth-Century British Methodism.* Lanham, MD: Scarecrow Press, 2008.

Scougal, Henry. *The Life of God in the Soul of Man.* In Jebb, John. *Parish and Religious Family Library.* Vol. 10, *Piety without Asceticism; or, The Protestant Kempis. A Manual of Christian Faith and Practice Selected from the Writings of Scougal, Charles How, and Cudworth.* New York: Protestant Episcopal Press, 1831.

Scupoli, Dom Lorenzo. *The Spiritual Combat and a Treatise on Peace of Soul.* Rockford, IL: Tan Books, 1990.

Stokes, Stewart L. *The Life and Ministry of the Rev. George Whitefield: The Inspiration behind Old South, First Presbyterian Church and a Force behind the First Great Awakening.* Newburyport, MA: Historical Committee of Old South First Presbyterian Church, 2011.

Stout, Harry S. *The Divine Dramatist: George Whitefield and the Rise of Modern Evangelicalism.* Grand Rapids: Eerdmans, 1991.

Tyerman, Luke. *The Life of George Whitefield,* 2 vols. London: Hodder & Stoughton, 1890.

Whitefield, George. *Journals.* Carlisle, PA: Banner of Truth, 1992.

———. *Letters, 1734–1742.* Carlisle, PA: Banner of Truth, 1976.

———. *Select Sermons of George Whitefield.* Carlisle, PA: Banner of Truth, 1990.

———. "Sermons of the Reverend George Whitefield." Center for Reformed Theology and Apologetics. http://www.reformed.org/documents/index.html?mainframe=http://www.reformed.org/documents/Whitefield.html.

INDEX OF SUBJECTS AND NAMES

Arminianism, 73, 94, 96, 118, 176

Articles of Religion of the Church of England, 34, 42, 44, 75–76, 118, 122, 135

Bell Inn, 13, 16, 26–28, 31–32, 84, 107

Bethesda, 51–53, 67, 74, 86, 90, 102, 189

Boston, Massachusetts, 61, 66, 91, 100

Bristol, England, 19, 25, 31, 36, 50, 84, 114

Calvinism, 64, 73, 82, 87, 94, 96, 176

Church of England, 13, 17, 18, 40, 41–42, 44–46, 48, 51, 57, 63–64, 72, 83, 84, 87, 102, 125, 135, 154

Davies, Samuel, 55, 57–58

Dissenting tradition, 42, 44–45, 51, 57, 59, 63, 74, 84, 102

Edwards, Jonathan, 55, 56, 58–59, 64, 114, 132, 133, 189

election, 60, 63, 73–77, 83, 96, 112, 114–15, 116–30, 132, 134, 135, 176, 179

Erskine, Ebenezer, 18, 82–83

Erskine, Ralph, 18, 82–83

field preaching, 20, 26, 49–51, 59, 61, 69, 72, 82, 91–92, 101, 190

Foote, Samuel, 68–69

Franke, August Hermann, 37, 47

Franklin, Benjamin, 19, 55, 61–62, 78–82, 87, 102–3

free grace, 28, 56, 63, 74, 76–77, 84, 87, 96, 111, 114, 118, 125, 134, 135

Frelinghuysen, Theodore, 55, 56, 57, 59

Garrick, David, 69

Georgia, 15, 17, 40, 46–48, 51, 56, 72, 101, 115–16, 124, 181, 183, 189

Gloucester, England, 13, 16, 26, 27, 29–32, 39–40, 42, 45, 84, 94, 107, 180

Halle, Germany, 37, 47, 102

Harris, Howell, 77, 82

Hastings, Selina (Countess of Huntingdon), 19, 85–87, 98
Holy Club, 35, 38, 40, 46, 71

Log College, 56–57
London, England, 20, 26, 43–45, 48, 69, 86, 90, 115–16, 124, 183–84

Newburyport, Massachusetts, 20, 66, 92, 94, 99, 103
newspapers, 18–19, 61, 79–80, 85, 87, 95, 100, 189

Old South (Presbyterian) Church, 66, 92, 98, 100, 103
Oxford, 16–17, 21, 25, 29, 32, 33–37, 39, 40, 43, 45–46, 48, 71, 109, 181, 183

Parsons, Jonathan, 92–93
Pemberton, Ebenezer, 92–93
Pembroke College, 16, 20, 32, 35, 37, 40, 109
perseverance of the saints, 63, 73–74, 75, 83, 117, 120, 126, 166, 182
Philadelphia, Pennsylvania, 51, 61, 65, 80–81, 91, 93, 151
Pietism, 37, 46–47, 72, 87, 102

Reformed tradition, 20, 41, 56, 63, 82, 86, 102, 111, 166–67, 176

Revolution (American), 18, 55, 62, 64–65, 67, 189

Savannah, Georgia, 17, 46–48, 53, 56, 74, 85–86, 91, 93, 101–2
sermons, 18–19, 20, 26, 42–43, 44, 51, 57, 58, 60–62, 64–65, 67, 72, 74, 79, 80, 85, 86, 89–90, 92, 93–97, 100, 102–3, 111, 114–17, 122, 131–32, 134–35, 136–68, 169–85, 187–88, 190
slavery, 17, 52, 97, 103, 149
St. Mary de Crypt Church, 16, 30–31, 32, 42

Tennent, Gilbert, 55, 57
Tennent, William, 56–57
Tottenham Court Road Tabernacle, 86, 89, 93, 100

Wesley, Charles, 11, 17, 19, 20, 32, 34, 35–39, 40, 46, 71–72, 77, 78, 110
Wesley, John, 11, 17, 19, 20, 35–36, 39, 40, 46–47, 52, 71–78, 81–82, 84, 86, 93–97, 102, 110, 111–13, 117–19, 121–24, 128–29, 131, 134–35, 188
Wheatley, Phillis, 97–98
Whitefield, Elizabeth, 27–29, 31–32, 107–9
Whittier, John Greenleaf, 103–4

James L. Schwenk (M.Div., Evangelical Seminary; M.Phil. and Ph.D., Drew University) is the lead pastor of Gingrichs Mennonite Church in Lebanon, Pennsylvania. He has taught the history of Christianity at numerous schools, most recently at Evangelical Seminary in Myerstown, Pennsylvania, and at Zaporozhye Bible College and Seminary in Zaporozhye, Ukraine. His research interests include J. R. R. Tolkien, C. S. Lewis, and *Doctor Who*.

Also in the GUIDED TOUR series

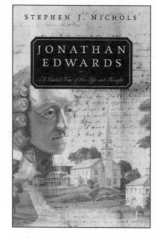

by Stephen J. Nichols
Price: $14.99
To order, visit
www.prpbooks.com
or call
1(800) 631-0094

"A lively and vivid introduction to America's greatest theologian—the best one yet for use in most churches and Christian colleges."

—DOUGLAS A. SWEENEY

"Nichols is an enthusiastic, experienced, and reliable tour guide to the theology of Jonathan Edwards. If your experience is like mine, these pages will make you want to visit Edwards on your own for frequent and extended periods. An excellent introduction."

—SINCLAIR FERGUSON

"Edwards is still America's greatest theologian, and his works remain of lasting value to the church. This book is a useful introduction to the great man's message and ministry. Nichols has chosen his material carefully to help readers begin to understand Edwards's most important writings."

—PHILIP GRAHAM RYKEN

Also in the Guided Tour *series*

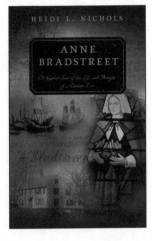

by Heidi L. Nichols
Price: $13.99
To order, visit
www.prpbooks.com
or call
1(800) 631-0094

"This book does a masterful job of performing the task identified in the subtitle—it is a guided tour of the life and work of Anne Bradstreet, conducted by a wonderfully talented tour guide. For anyone wishing to acquire or renew an acquaintance with Anne Bradstreet, this is the book of choice."

— Leland Ryken

"Puritan pioneer Anne Bradstreet, solid believer, ardent wife, faithful mother, wise woman, and gifted poetess, is a lady well worth meeting. Dr. Nichols arranges that meeting beautifully in these pages, and merits our gratitude for doing so."

— J. I. Packer

"Nichols not only illuminates the poet's life and social context, she makes it possible for a new generation to savor Anne Bradstreet's own words and to share the sorrows, joy, and hope of her inner journey."

— Charles Hambrick-Stowe

Also in the GUIDED TOUR *series*

by Stephen J. Nichols
Price: $13.99
To order, visit
www.prpbooks.com
or call
1(800) 631-0094

"For over half a century Roland Bainton's *Here I Stand* has been the best popular introduction to Luther. Stephen Nichols's engaging volume is in many ways better than Bainton's for this purpose. It deserves to be widely read, and as an unashamed Luther-lover I hope it will be."

—J. I. PACKER

"How do you do a book on everything from training children to hymns to preaching to political conflict—and have it running over with the glorious gospel? Nichols has done it. Be alert: people forget how life-changing the gospel really is—and then are astonished to remember it again as they read Luther."

—D. CLAIR DAVIS

"Since Luther published a printed work about every two weeks of his adult life, there is a lot of ground to cover. But Nichols knows the terrain well and opens up its treasures with a deft touch."

—MARK NOLL

Also in the GUIDED TOUR *series*

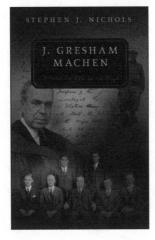

by Stephen J. Nichols
Price: $13.99
To order, visit
www.prpbooks.com
or call
1(800) 631-0094

"Nichols has done a fine job of presenting an accessible introduction to the life and thought of J. Gresham Machen. Nichols offers lucid expositions and fresh interpretations based on his own research."
—GEORGE M. MARSDEN

"J. Gresham Machen's writing was as clear as his arguments were persuasive. Nichols has accomplished the rare feat of making Machen even more accessible. For readers unfamiliar with Machen, this is the perfect appetizer to the feast of further study in Machen's writings. For those more knowledgeable, this will be a reliable reference."
—D. G. HART

"Nichols has provided an accessible gateway to conservative Presbyterianism's most stalwart defender in the tumultuous 1920s. His admiring portrait reminds us of Machen's probing scholarship, his trenchant analysis of modernism, and his attempts to further the Christian world and life view in American culture."
—ANDREW HOFFECKER